D1556040

TANZANIA

TANZANIA

PORTRAIT OF A NATION

Photographs by
Paul Joynson-Hicks

Introductions by
Eric Sikujua Ng'maryo

Quiller Press

For

Jamie and Jack Banks
my great and wonderful nephews

Copyright © 1998 Paul Joynson-Hicks
Introduction Text Copyright © 1998 Eric Ng'maryo
Two photographs on page 40 Copyright © 1998 Frank Teuling

The author has asserted his right under the Copyright, Designs
and Patents Act 1988 to be identified as Author of this work.

First published 1998 by
Quiller Press Ltd
46 Lillie Road
London SW6 1TN

ISBN 1 899163 37 9

All rights reserved.
No part of this work may be reproduced by any means
without the prior written permission of the publishers.

Designed by Jo Lee
Front cover picture: Bismarck Rock, Tanzania
Colour reproduction by Unifoto International, Cape Town.
Printed by South Sea International Press Limited, Hong Kong.

Contents

Acknowledgements

It is absolutely impossible to put a book together like this without the help of loads of different people. I am deeply grateful to everyone. I see this book as a joint effort between all of us; we've got the same idea in mind – let's produce something which shows a bit more of Tanzania than what has already been seen. So all I can do is convey my deep-felt thanks to you all and hope that I have succeeded. Here are the names of most of you who have helped, though it is not unlikely I may have left someone out – being as absent-minded as I am – so, if I have, please tell me or write to me and I will specially dedicate a book to you. There are so many of you who have helped in so many wonderful ways that I will try to mention everyone in the order I went through the country:

I will start with the person who probably deserves a sainthood, a man who put up with me for months on end, a genius when it comes to fixing and maintaining Landrovers, the best driver in the world and someone on whom I depended time and time again and who has never failed me – my friend Herman Lyatuu. Then without the backing and support of Jeremy Lefroy and the African Coffee Company, the whole project would not have got off the ground. Everything was made possible by them and I am deeply grateful. Thanks go to Eric Ng'maryo for his excellent introduction text and regional intros – brilliant. In the UK many thanks to my great family: Gill and Crispin Brentford, Emma J H, Ro, Si, Jack and Jamie Banks, and Amy J H. They, as always, were fully behind me and helped and supported me in many different ways. I also owe a deep debt of gratitude to the Tanzanian authorities who facilitated the various bits and pieces required. At the Tanzanian Tourist Board, Credo Sinyangwe, Managing Director and Peter Mwenguo, Director of Marketing; in the Immigration Department thanks to the Director KWD Kihomano and Vicky Lembeli; at Tanzania National Parks, thanks to Mr Bigurube and Diocless Emmanuel; in the Ngorongoro Conservation Area, my thanks to Lazaro Mariki, Saning'o K Ole Telele and Mama Lujuo.

In Moshi, where I was based, a few very kind people really looked after me. I was always made incredibly welcome in their homes which made my short stays between trips immensely enjoyable: a very special thanks to Janet, Ben and Eliza Lefroy for feeding me and generally putting up with me so often and another very special thanks to Ralph and Bente Medoch for the endless champagne, great food and even better company, Robert (don't mention the 18th at Limuru) Heuveldop, Uli Doring (many thanks to Uli for his great intro to Tarangire NP) and Judith, Sief and Ida

Van der Salm and Clive Ashton. A big thanks to Ally Suleiman who looked after me at home in Moshi – a great cook whether at home or in the bush. Still in Moshi, my thanks to Chuni's Garage, which did an excellent job renewing the engine of my Landrover and thus extending its life immensely. My special thanks to Brian and Sheila Mason and Jon and Jo Salmon who have looked after me wonderfully whenever I have been in Dar es Salaam. Also thanks to all at Aleria Enterprises for all their help and use of their office.

While I was travelling, some people very kindly put me up in their superb lodges and camps. Thank you all very much; I really appreciated your support and kind hospitality. If anyone reads this and is planning to go to any of the parks containing these lodges and camps then they must stay there – they are indisputably the best. In Tarangire NP - the Tarangire Safari Lodge – thanks to Steve and Marilyn and Jon and Annette Simonson; in Mahale Mountains NP – the Mahale Mountains Tented Camp; and in Katavi Plains NP – the Katavi Tented Camp – thanks to Roland and Zoe Purcell (and Simon Duman in Mahale) and also thanks for the flights in his great plane and for Roland and Zoe's inspired introductions to Mahale and Katavi. In the Selous at Mbuyu Camp, thanks go to Alfred Moser; in Ruaha NP, to Geoff Fox and Justin Short for my stay in the Ruaha River Lodge; and an extra thank you to Geoff and Vicky Fox for their kind hospitality and help in Mufindi. Thanks also to Tony and Lucy Fitzjohn for their kind hospitality and help in Mkomazi Game Reserve and their superb introduction. Also to those at Serengeti Balloon Safaris: Joe Gilles, Michel Theolier and Tony Pascoe. Ballooning – a great trip strongly to be recommended.

There are many of you who helped with local information and cups of reviving tea, food and general kindness. Many thanks to you all: Dr Philip Setel, for his inspiration and ideas at the very beginning, Anne Outwater for her general info on TZ, Ingolf and Bente Morch on Sumbawanga and Kalambo Falls, to all at Brooke Bond Tea in Mufindi, Mrs Chrissie Edwards on Mbeya, Jim and Joyce Laird in Mbinga at the cathedral, John Acland at the Mwadui Diamond Mine, Simon Trevor and Lissa Reuben in Ruaha, Marcus Borner, Grant Peyton, Ian and Gizzy in the Serengeti, Peter Jones and Eric Ng'maryo for letting me stay at M'Simbati and to Derek 'Jock' Wilson and Ian Horsefall of Frontier Tanzania for their kind hospitality there, Tim and Rachel Fowler on Mtwara, Father Ildephons on the Makonde carvers and an intro to Hendrix, Dr. Ole Kuney for

his info and introductions to the Maasai, Chris and Nani Schmeling at Lake Eyasi, Graham Anderson in Amani. In Zanzibar, I thank Mark Wheeler, Jon Perry, Andy Williams, Lucy and Abby Worsnip and Neil Mortimer for their kind hospitality, information and great company; also Nancy Galloway for all her info on the islands, and Madawa who showed us around his place, the island and his workshop and for his info on Pemba island. On Mafia Island, my thanks to Jean and Anne de Villiers. Also many thanks to Neil and Liz Baker for all their help in editing out all my ferocious blunders.

In the UK, my sincere thanks to Annie Sutherland, a brilliant super-gifted person and writer who scribed the excellent National Park introductions. Also to Robert and Vanessa Fairer who have helped in innumerable ways, especially taking the time with the editing and duping, without whom the book would probably contain several thousand pictures! My thanks to Simon Larkin for his great writing on the refugee camps in TZ. More thanks go to Metro Imaging, the photo company of photo companies, and to Charlotte Wylie and all the guys at 3 Jubilee Place for doing such a good job. I also must say thanks to Gray Levett at Grays of Westminster, the ultimate Nikon shop, for all his friendly advice and help and supply of my kit. Also to Alliance Air for their support of the project, particularly Adam Roberts and Vicky Ross in the air and Bree Sims in London. There are two books which have helped greatly throughout the year: (i) Richard Despard Estes: *The Behaviour Guide to African Mammals* (which my mother, I have since learned, may be buying to learn more about me!) - an invaluable guide to the animals you see around the parks of TZ. (ii) The *Bradt Guide to Tanzania*, brilliantly written by Philip Briggs, another invaluable guide to the whole country. I must also express my appreciation to the National Park guide books on many of the parks. They are concise, helpful and full of loads of great information and drawings. The guides are published in conjunction with the African Wildlife Foundation and my thanks go to the contributors Jeanette Hanby, Deborah Snelson and the brilliant illustrators David Bygott and Jonathan Scott. Many thanks also to Frank Teuling for his great pictures of the rhino sanctuary in Mkomazi Game Reserve.

An enormous thanks also to James Lanaway at Bausch and Lomb for supplying me with such excellent Ray-Ban sunglasses.

Lastly, I must say a huge thank you to my publisher, Jeremy Greenwood, and to the highly talented designer who put this book together, Jo Lee.

Introduction

In the great temple of Thebes at Karnak, on one of its pillars, a celebration of a man called Seneb is recorded. Seneb was from a land known as Punt-Punt or, more correctly, Pwnt-Pwnt. Hieroglyphics express only the consonantal skeleton of a word, without vowels. Pwnt-Pwnt could thus be pronounced "Pwani-Pwani", words which, even in modern day Swahili, mean "shoreline" or "coast".

The time of the record is about 2050 BC and Punt-Punt had already been, for almost a thousand years, a well-known source for myrrh and incense, two sweet-swelling substances that were widely used in religious rites of the Ancient Egyptians. Other exotic exports from Punt-Punt to Ancient Egypt included ivory, tortoise shell, rhinoceros horn, gum copal, leopard skins, ebony, ambergis, palm oil and beeswax. One's imagination may well go back four thousand years to picture this distinguished East African, possibly from Tanzania, impressing the Thebans enough to have his name inscribed in a temple for their official state god.

The Tanzanian coast, and further north up to the Horn of Africa, can boast a tradition of commerce with the rest of the world that goes back five thousand years. It is obvious that after the time of Seneb this coast continued to remain crucial to traders and seafarers plying the Indian Ocean and the Red Sea. Around 100 AD, a Greek mariner form Alexandria wrote the famous *Periplous of the Erythræn Sea*. This book was a guide to merchant-sailors to the Red Sea and western Indian Ocean (which was, at that time, known as the "Erythræn Sea") and makes copious reference to the already ancient trade between what was originally Punt-Punt (and was, at this time, called Azania) and such divergent and far-off places as China, India, Arabia, Egypt and the ancient Mediterranean world. The *Periplous* mentions the town of Rhapta, the capital of Azania. Although the site for Rhapta has not been positively identified, historians have suggested that it could have been situated near the mouth of the River Rufiji. The *Periplous* describes the people of Azania as tall and piratical; at this time, a small population of Arabs (most probably from Himyar, in south-western Arabia) had already learned the local language, taken Azanian women in marriage and

settled on the coast, intermingling with the locals.

About the same time, Indonesians had found their way to what is now called Malagasy and, easily crossing the 400km of the Mozambique Channel with their outrigger canoes, had found their way to the Mozambican and Tanzanian coasts. If these intrepid sailors did not leave great monuments or noticeable descendants in Tanzania, they did introduce the banana, a food crop that was later to be adopted and aggressively cultivated in several places in the country.

The interior of Tanzania has a history almost a thousand times older than that of the coast. It was the cradle-land and home of the famous *Zinjanthropus* of the genus *Australopithecus boisei*. *Australopithecus* has been described as a "cousin" of man. A nearer "cousin" of the human being was *Homo habilis* (skilled human), also found in Tanzania.

Whereas *Australopithecus* has a bigger hominid stature with a less developed cranium, *Homo habilis* has a bigger cranium and was skilled in making tools. This hominid also had a very human-looking hand and foot. These two "cousins" of ours are thought to have lived about 1,750,000 years ago. Around half a million years later, the *Homo erectus (Pithecanthropus)* evolved. Present human beings (*Homo sapiens*) may be descended from the *Homo erectus*.

The Olduvai Gorge is known for its incredible archaeological wealth. It is said that in 1911, a German entomologist, Professor Kanttwinkel, was chasing a rare butterfly in the south-eastern Serengeti plains. Not looking where he was going and focused only on his exotic find, the Professor nearly fell to his death off a sheer cliff. The Professor lost the butterfly. When he explored the treacherous cliff face, the Professor saw fossil bones sticking out of the rock. He reported this to his colleagues in Berlin and it was in this way that Olduvai (in Maasai meaning "the place of the sansevieria plants") came to be a world-famous archaeological site.

It is in the Olduvai Gorge that in 1959 Louis Leakey and his team found the skull of *Zinjanthropus*, and it is in the same place that the bones of *Homo habilis* and *Homo erectus* as well as their tools were found. After the death of Leakey in 1972, his wife, Mary Leakey, continued with

the archaeological research. In 1976, her assistant, Peter Jones, and her son, Philip, noticed what they believed to be a trail of hominid footprints. This was at Laetoeli, about thirty kilometres east of the Ngorongoro Crater and south of the Olduvai Gorge. Few finds in archaeology bring to us prehistory in a more immediate and poignant way.

The time is 3,600,000 years ago, in the Pliocene period, and the rainy season is approaching. Sunshine has been dulled by a slight drizzle. To the east, a volcano now known as Sadiman rumbles and belches, billowing dark clouds of volcanic dust and smoke. This drifts and settles at Laetoli. As is common even today, the drizzle goes. The sun shines hazily through the volcanic smog and after some time it drizzles again. The land stretches on, dotted with vegetation that would be familiar even today: *Acacia tortilis*, whistling thorn, prickly bushes. There is great abundance of wildlife, some of which is now extinct. Guinea fowl and ostriches walk about without fear. Prehistoric elephants go about their business. Giraffes browse the tops of trees covered with volcanic dust, which they don't seem to mind. A hare dashes from one bush to another. Then two hominids appear, walking closely together; a male and a female, coming from the south. The male walks slightly in front, carrying the dead branch of a tree.

The female follows, heavily pregnant. The male looks back occasionally, grunting encouragement. The female checks the nearby bushes with alert eyes, more sensitive to danger than the male. The male looks back again and makes a soft, sibilant noise. The female bares her teeth in a smile.

And so they pass among the animals at a permissible distance, going to the north and disappearing behind a clump of trees. The footprints of the two hominids as well as the tracks of the many animals, birds and even insects of that day are well marked on the damp volcanic ash.

The sun then shines and the tracks dry. Sadiman heaves out more smoke and ash which gently settles on Laetoli, covering the footprints and tracks. Another drizzle, then sunshine again. That brief period of time, perhaps just an afternoon, is preserved for 3,600,000 years in the ash of Laetoli, where Peter Jones and Philip Leakey came across it in 1976.

North-eastern Tanzania, in particular the area comprising Olduvai, Engaruka and Kondoa, is perhaps the richest and the most rewarding area in archaeology. Fossilised human and animal remains, stone implements, including cutting tools, artefacts and rock paintings have outlined Tanzania's prehistory. It is, in all likelihood, the prehistory of human beings from the early Stone Age (1,500,000 years ago) to the middle Stone Age (125,000 years ago) to the late Stone Age (15,000 years ago) when *Homo sapiens* appeared, to the Iron Age (3000 years ago). Food production through agriculture and pastoralism began at about the same time as the Iron Age.

Sorghum and millet probably came to Tanzania from Ethiopia about 2000 years ago; at around the same time, bananas, rice, yams, and coconuts may have reached Tanzania from South-East Asia by way of the Indian Ocean, most likely via Malagasy. Maize and cassava are relatively recent crops in Tanzania. These were introduced to West Africa from the Americas and reached Tanzania 400 to 500 years ago. Cattle, sheep and goats appear to have moved to Tanzania from North and West Africa.

The earliest known iron workings in the early Iron Age are in the area around Lake Victoria. The people who manufactured the iron also produced distinctive pottery known as Urewe ware. The earliest Urewe site is in Kagera region. The Urewe culture was already well-established around 500 BC Urewe excavations by Peter Schmidt have shown evidence of the production of steel-like metal with high carbon content centuries before a similar quality of iron was produced in Europe.

Urewe iron culture spread quickly over eastern and southern Africa, reaching the eastern parts of Zambia and Zimbabwe by 300 AD and South Africa and southern Congo by 500 AD.

Historians believe that the rapid spread of Iron Age technology in East and Central Africa coincided with the dispersal of the Bantu people who occupy most of Tanzania today. The word "bantu" means "people" or "human beings" and is pronounced in a recognisably similar way by all the Bantu speakers.

Linguistic analysis and archaeology have established the original dispersal area of the Bantu people to be the southern Cameroon area of West Africa. From here, two streams moved through the Congo rain forest eastwards and southwards. Another stream avoided the rain forest and moved along its northern fringe eastwards

up to the Sudan and southwards to Lake Victoria. These Bantu ancestors established the Urewe early Iron Age culture, whence further movements took them to the east and south of Tanzania and to central and southern Africa. Other streams of Bantu people entered Tanzania through the land openings between Lake Victoria and Lake Tanganyika and between Lake Tanganyika and Lake Nyasa. Thus, by the fourth century AD most of the ethnic groups existing in Tanzania today had already settled in the country. In the process they had assimilated most of the scattered populations of Khoikhoi and Cushitic peoples who had entered the country 2000 years before.

When speaking of dispersal and movement of the Bantu people, one should not think of mass migration. Rather, the process was slow and of small scale movement over many years. Groups formed and groups disbanded; people absorbed other people and they were in turn absorbed; clans displaced other clans; and disease, famine, drought, floods, locust invasions and wars took a toll on populations while at the same time pushing them on to better lands and better times.

This movement of people continued well into recent times. Between 1700 AD and 1800 AD for example, the Maasai, a Nilotic group of pastoralists, moved from Kenya into northern Tanzania and as far south as Dodoma. Over the years they have moved further south and east and are now in Iringa, Morogoro and even Ruvuma regions.

The Ngoni, fleeing from the *mfecane* ("the times of troubles") brought about by the Zulu expansion under their famous king, Shaka, entered south-western Tanzania in a large army led by Zwengendaba. This was in 1840. They conquered the Fipa people and settled. Another militant group led by Maseko came to Tanzania up the eastern side of Lake Nyasa and settled in Songea, having defeated and absorbed the Yao people. From these two groups, several dispersals took place. The Tuta moved from Ufipa northwards and settled in north-west Tanzania. The Gwangara also moved from Ufipa to Songea, where they fought fierce battles with the Maseko and, defeated, went southwards across the Ruvuma river under the leadership of Maputo. Others fled northwards to Morogoro where they settled and called themselves the Mbunga.

The history of the people of Tanzania is thus the history of movement, and the most immediate consequence of this was trade. As people moved, they took with them what was valuable: iron implements, grain, items of clothing and decoration. Naturally, it was very hard for a group

of people to be able to produce everything they needed. Alternatively, people found themselves with goods that were in excess of their needs, and the sensible option was to exchange what was in excess with what was not available or immediately needed. This was the beginning of barter trade. Agricultural produce, iron weapons and implements, pottery, dried fish, livestock, milk, salt, honey and beeswax as well as items of decoration were just some of the many goods that were exchanged between people and communities throughout Tanzania. Agricultural communities would probably not have enough livestock or iron implements and they bartered their grain and other produce for these valuable items. Fishermen traded dried fish for pots. Salt was exchanged for beeswax which was used for waxing drumskins and bowstrings. Items which were in great need, or which were easy to take from one point to another, took the form of currency. Thus, salt, iron hoes and livestock started being used as money.

As communities grew and became more permanent, trade went beyond things that were immediately needed by the traders. Now people speculated on things that were likely to be needed by other people. A person would barter his iron hoes for salt, not because he needed the salt, but because the people in a place three or four villages beyond greatly needed salt and this would trade better than his hoes. It was this sort of speculation that brought about the 'chain' trade that linked people who lived many walking months apart. It was also this chain trade that brought to the coast items that were found or produced a long way in the interior of the country.

The caravan routes that began to be organised from the Tanzanian coast in the mid 1800s used the routes that had been established by chain trade between settlements and peoples over hundreds of years. It was these same people from the interior who provided the links that could, for example, make it possible for the Baganda in the reign of Kabaka Kyabagu (c. 1760) to have procelain cups and plates produced overseas. These very routes were later to be faithfully followed by the railways and roads that the Germans and the British built.

There is a saying that good trade is when the buyer believes he has ripped off the seller and the seller thinks the converse is the case. This was what happened when overseas trade extended into the interior of Tanzania. The major item of that trade was ivory. Ivory trade far exceeded the trade in slaves in importance and it can be said that it was mainly the demand for ivory that stimulated the slave trade in the interior of Tanzania. Guns that hunted elephants were also used in capturing slaves, and the slaves that were captured and taken to the coast were convenient carriers of ivory.

By the end of the 18th century, and with the subsequent introduction of firearms, the coastal elephant population was severely depleted and people further inland became aware of the trading value of ivory at the coast. Ivory was in great demand in India, where married women were expected to wear ivory bangles – which were buried with them when they died. Indian carvers bought ivory and used it to produce figurines and other art pieces. Japan required ivory for production of *netsukes,* which are ivory buttons used to suspend objects from a belt. In Europe, ivory was needed for the rising class of luxury-loving bourgeoisie and it was a sign of distinction and wealth to have ivory-handled cuttlery, ivory combs, napkin rings, snuff boxes and letter openers, to mention only a few of such items. Ivory was also used to make chessmen, billiard balls and piano keys. In 1859, for example, 220 tonnes of ivory were exported through Zanzibar, mainly to Europe, India and the Far East.

It was the great demand for ivory that transformed the chain trade to long distance trade. Whereas the chain trade was carried from person to person and from community to community, with the long distance trade, goods took off directly from their point of origin to the coast by being carried all the way by porters and slaves.

For the people of the interior of Tanzania at that time, ivory was of more or less the same value as the bones of an elephant. An elephant was killed for meat or for a show of courage and no-one gave any particular importance to the ivory. Some people, like the Nyamwezi, used ivory to make bangles; and ivory may have been used by other people to make ritual objects. There was therefore a deep sense of satisfaction when it was discovered that this item was deeply coveted by the people of the coast and could be exchanged for generous quantities of items such as iron implements, copper wire, salt, beads, cloth and, even more importantly, firearms that had unique advantages in war and were capable of killing elephants and generating even more ivory.

The Yao, the Nyamwezi and the Gogo were spirited long distance traders; and the Kamba of Kenya could travel from Mombasa past Kilimanjaro, across the Rift Valley to Lake Victoria, southwards to Urambo and Tabora and to the southern tip of Lake Tanganyika to trade with the Fipa and the Bemba of Zambia before turning back again to the coast.

Long distance ivory trade went hand in hand with the slave trade. Slaves were required for clove plantations in Zanzibar and Pemba, and in the French sugar cane plantations in Mauritius and Reunion. Other slaves were exported to the Persian Gulf and the Americas. By 1840s, it is estimated that 20,000 slaves were sold yearly at Zanzibar, this figure increasing considerably in the next two or three decades.

The odious nature of the slave trade and the human suffering it caused has been narrated many times. Like the Nguni invasions (which were contemporaneous with the height of the trade), the slave trade brought about depopulation, break up of community life, famine and listlessness. The people who suffered most were those living in small, peaceable communities. On the other hand, the better organised and more war-like groups benefited from the trade by raiding their neighbours and adding to their armouries. They became better organised and had a marked political advantage when German colonists came in the wake of the ivory and slave traders.

The present-day boundaries of Tanzania may have been the result of Anglo-German colonial rivalries and machinations, but within those borders the kernel of national unity was already alive and obviously present. This kernel was the result of centuries of trade, marriage, long distance travel, cultural and technological exchange as well as struggle and warfare among the people who were later to be put together within boundaries drawn by indifferent strangers scheming and bargaining in meeting rooms on another continent thousands of kilometres away. This was part of the so-called scramble for Africa.

In the November 1884, three young Germans arrived in Zanzibar. Ardent members of the newly formed Society for German Colonisation, they kept their mission a secret and disguised themselves as mechanics. Their leader was Carl Peters, a man who would later earn the epithet "*Mkono wa Damu*", which is the Swahili for "the man with the blood-stained hands". Peters and his friends seem to have been able to obtain within the short period of six weeks signed "treaties" with the chiefs of the area between Pangani and Rufiji Rivers. Returning to Zanzibar, Peters claimed to have protectorates over the chiefdoms of Ungara, Unguru, Uzigua and Ukami; and that the chiefs of these areas had ceded their territories to him. The Sultan of Zanzibar's lame remonstrations to the British about losing his rights over what Carl Peters "took" were unheeded. Peters returned to Berlin in February 1885 and within a month, the German Government under Chancellor Otto Bismarck-Schönhausen used Peters' "protectorates" as a basis for the establishment of a German Protectorate. In 1888 the Germans bought from the Sultan of Zanzibar the 10 mile strip (which was all that remained of Zanzibar's claim to influence on the mainland) for 400,000 Marks. The strip extended from the River Ruvuma past Mombasa to Witu, near the mouth of the River Tana.

German colonialism in Tanzania was met with a series of uprisings and resitance beginning with caravan leaders such as Abushiri of Pangani and those who supported him, and went as far south as Kilwa. It took a German officer, Major von Wissmann, together with a recruited contingent of 600 Nubians, 50 Somalis, 350 Zulus and 20 Turkish police to overwhelm Abushiri. The caravan leader had run short of manpower and provisions, and had to take refuge in Usagara. There he was captured and was hanged at Bagamoyo in 1889. Another resistance leader was Bwana Heri of Saadani. He was overcome by the Germans in 1890, and also hanged.

The Germans clashed with the Hehe people because their great leader, Mkwawa, had blocked the central caravan route to the coast from Tabora. Since the Germans depended on this route to reach the interior, they sent a force of 1000 soldiers whom Mkwawa soundly defeated. He was free of the Germans for three years and used the time to fortify his capital at Kalenga. In 1894 the Germans attacked it with a large expedition and, although they managed to capture it, Mkwawa escaped and carried on a guerilla campaign for another four years. When facing capture by the Germans, he shot himself rather than fall in the hands of his enemies. The Germans cut off his head and sent it to Germany. Persistent demands were made by the Hehe for its return but it was not until 1954 that this was done.

Further uprisings occurred among the Yao and the Gogo, and the chief in Ujiji, Tagarala, rose against the Germans. They were all defeated. The Germans imposed tax, usually in the form of a hut tax of three rupees per hut. In 1899, the first year of German taxation, 1651 rupees were paid in cash, 706 in kind, and 21,209 rupees in labour given by 7000 men. In 1902 the Germans compelled the people of each village in the Rufiji area to grow cotton as a cash crop. The cotton project was enforced with great brutality until the people could stand it no longer. There came a medicineman called Kinjekitile son of Ngwale of the village of Ngarambe. Kinjekitile became recognized as the mouthpiece of Bokero, a well known deity. By sprinkling people with a special water (*maji*), the prophet promised immunity against any evil. Inspired by Kinjekitile, the Ngindo and Pogoro people started what was later to be called the Maji Maji uprising in July 1905.

The rebellion brought together the people of the whole of southern Tanzania, making it the country's biggest violent mass movement for independence.

Kinjekitile became the prophet of Maji Maji and declared that his magic would turn German bullets into water. The movement swelled under the new faith of invincibility and soon the Bena, Ngoni, Mbunga, Zaramo, Pogoro, Ngindo and many others were fighting against the Germans. The uprising caught the German government unprepared and the Germans suffered heavy losses before they could counterattack. After much fighting, the myth of bullets turning to water was dispelled by the superiority of German weapons, and in a matter of months the uprising was suppressed. The leaders of the uprising were arrested and hanged, and to stop further resistance, the Germans applied a scorched earth policy on the entire Maji Maji area. Villages were destroyed, families broken up and crops in the fields put to the torch. There was a terrible famine that lasted for three years – called the Fugafuga. The exact death toll of the Maji Maji insurgents will never be known, but it has been estimated at between 250,000 and 300,000. For an area that was sparsely populated in the first place and was subsequently devastated by slave raiding and the Nguni invasion, this death toll could have taken up to half of the adult population.

The reasons the German Colonial Department ascribed to the Maji Maji uprising were the compulsory cotton scheme and the viciousness with which it was enforced. Baron Freiherr von Rechenberg was appointed Governor of German East Africa from 1906 to 1912. Rechenberg's policies were clearly aimed at reconciling and healing the effects of the uprising.

_____

The Maji Maji uprising and its suppression taught the Germans that there was a limit to the ill treatment of their East African subjects. To the people, the period of colonial rule had begun. There would be taxation, cultivation of crops that were not of any use to them, work in plantations they never owned, and acquisition of a religion and a system of justice they had never known before. There would also be education in the conqueror's skills and culture, and this would lead to acceptance and advancement in the society of the new overlords. Both the colonialists and the subjects learnt these lessons very quickly.

By the time the First World War broke out in 1914, sisal had already been established in what is now mainland Tanzania. Sisal had first been imported from Florida in the USA in 1892 and by 1914 it had become the main plantation crop grown by the majority of the 100 or so settler families in the country. Swahili, which had previously been a language of trade and long distance travel, became the language of the administration, the courts and the churches.

The new crops and plants that were brought into the country by the Germans are basically what we have today. The Germans' Amani agricultural and medical research centre in the Usambara mountains is still there today. As early as the 1890s hospitals run by German missionary doctors were established in Bumbuli in the Usambaras, in Morogoro and in Kilimanjaro. In 1891, cinchona trees were grown for quinine, which was used as a malaria prophylactic, and it was a German scientist, Dr. R. Koch, who associated sleeping sickness and its bovine equivalent, trypanosomiasis, with the tsetse fly. Likewise, Dr. Koch identified the tick as the cause for the cattle diseases of Tick fever and East Coast fever. The Germans also established health regulations against the spread of intestinal diseases. Encouragement of Indian traders and merchants to set up stores and businesses in the country was taken as the official policy of the German administration. Allidina Visram, a wealthy and enterprising Indian who started in Bagamoyo in 1877, managed to open stores in almost every German and British administrative centre in East Africa.

The Germans were keen to develop a transport system in their vast colony. The Usambara railway line was the first to be built. It started from Tanga in 1893 and by 1905 it reached Mombo. The extension of that line to Moshi was completed in 1912. Construction of the central line began from Dar es salaam in 1905 reaching Tabora in 1912 and Kigoma in 1914. Many roads linking upcountry administration and trading posts to the two railway lines were made in the same period.

Historians have noted that the economic infrastructure laid down by the Germans by 1914 was not greatly changed by the forty-five years of British administration. Lines of communications, towns, land areas set aside for plantations and the kinds of crops grown in the different areas of this country from those days have generally remained unchanged to this day.

_____

The First World War, dubbed "the war to end wars", was an European struggle between European powers for domination of the European continent. Yet that struggle had far reaching consequences for the people of the then German East Africa. When the war broke out in August 1914, the hope prevailing in Europe was that the "overseas possessions" of Britain and Germany would not be drawn into the war. However, the importance of Britain's African colonies called for a pre-emptive strike on the Germans in East Africa, and the Germans saw the usefulness of engaging the British in a war of attrition that would keep their East African forces and resources from the war in Europe.

And so the war was fought, mainly in German East Africa, opening with the British naval attacks on Dar es Salaam and Tanga. German forces were under their legendary commander, General Paul von Lettow-Vorbeck. In answer to the attacks on the two coastal towns, von Lettow-Vorbeck and his men, numbering less that 3000, moved to Kilimanjaro and carried out raids on the Uganda railway across the border at Taveta.

Despite the additional forces from British India, a seaborne attack in January, 1915 on Tanga failed. In July 1915 the German cruiser, the *Konigsberg*, was destroyed in the Rufiji delta. At this point, the British navy was in control of the coastal waters, and the Germans were unable to get supplies from overseas. When South African troops under General Smuts arrived at the beginning of 1916, General von Lettow-Vorbeck was driven out of Kilimanjaro down to the Ruvu River. Skilfully manoeuvring, the German General kept the British, South African, Rhodesian, Nyasaland and Belgian forces busy until the end of 1917 when the Germans were forced out of the country into Mozambique. Von Lettow-Vorbeck continued fighting, attacking Northern Rhodesia and evading both defeat and capture until the Germans surrendered and the European conflict came to an end in November 1918.

German East Africa was totally devastated. The war had been fought with weapons and a ruthlessness that was almost unknown to the people of the colony, and since many had been taken as soldiers and and even more as porters in the so-called Carrier-Corps, the combat toll was great. Settler plantations had been abandoned and neglected and the fledgeling peasant cash crop and subsistence agriculture was in ruins. Commerce, particularly overseas trade, had come to a virtual standstill. This dire situation was worsened by a famine and an influenza epidemic that immediately followed the war. German East Africa was surrendered by the Germans and handed over to the newly formed League of Nations. On 22nd July 1922, the former colony was entrusted to the British, who were mandated to administer it and promote the material and moral well-being as well as social progress of its inhabitants. Annual reports on the progress made in the country were to be submitted to the Permanent Mandates Commission of the League of Nations. Thus the country, now renamed

Tanganyika, was from the very onset of British administration destined for self-rule and independence.

British administration over Tanganyika started with Sir Horace Byatt as Governor. The task of reconstructing the country's economy as well as the legal and administration system was truly formidable. Byatt had to make do with the remnants of the German administration. Sir Donald Cameron, Governor from 1925 to 1931, set a clearer course for administering Tanganyika.

Having worked in Nigeria under Frederick John Dealtry Lugard, the architect of indirect rule, Cameron established the governing of the people of Tanganyika through their own traditional institutions. However, unlike Nigeria and Uganda where there were strong traditional rulers and chiefs, Tanganyika did not have powerful rulers. In the end, therefore, chiefs who had been empowered by the British administration to maintain law and order, collect taxes and keep records of revenue and expenditure appeared to many of their own people to be agents of the protectorate government.

It was during the Cameron administration that Tanganyika started its slow recovery from the First World War. The railway line linking Mwanza to Tabora was completed in 1928, and in 1929 the Usambara railway line was extended from Moshi to Arusha. Settler plantations started production once again and, although German plantations had been confiscated and auctioned in 1922, Germans gradually trickled back so that, by the end of 1930, there were more German than British settlers in Tanganyika.

Peasant cash crop agriculture, particularly coffee in the Kilimanjaro and Arusha areas, caught on and grew rapidly, despite a deliberate government policy discouraging peasant cultivation of the crop. By 1933, there were 6,000,000 coffee trees in the area, and one-third of all families in Kilimanjaro were growing coffee. At this time, more than one half of all the coffee produced in Tanganyika was grown by Africans.

Cotton had equal success among small scale African farmers around Lake Victoria, and it was the success in cotton cultivation among African peasants that prompted the extension of the railway line from Tabora to Mwanza.

Out of the participation of small scale farmers in cultivation of cash crops, co-operative unions emerged. As early as 1925 the Kilimanjaro Native Planters' Association was formed in Kilimanjaro. Its objective was to market African-produced coffee on Kilimanjaro. This role was taken over in 1932 by the Kilimanjaro Native Co-operative Union (KNCU). In the south, the Ngoni-Matengo Co-operative Marketing Union was registered in 1936 to market fire-cured tobacco, and the Bukoba Co-operative Union was formed in 1950.

It was also around this time that welfare societies with no ethnic affiliation started being formed by the first generation of educated elite in Tanganyika. Martin Kayamba, the urbane and polished civil servant, was the founder member and first president of the Tanganyika Territory African Civil Service Association. The Association had been formed in 1922 with the principal object of uniting Christian and Muslim civil servants in the Tanga area and to help them improve themselves. It had its own newspaper and football team.

When a branch of the Association was formed in Dar es Salaam, it got the support of Donald Cameron, the Governor. It was members of the Dar es Salaam branch of the Tanganyika Territory African Civil Service Association who formed themselves into the Tanganyika African Association (TAA), and it was from TAA that Tanganyika African National Union (TANU) developed in 1954. The first president of TANU was Julius Kambarage Nyerere, then only 32. TANU was principally a nationalist political party, and its initial cardinal goal was Tanganyika's self-government and independence.

The co-operative movement was already out of it's infancy and people's organisations in the welfare and trade union fields were rapidly transforming themselves into a concerted political force. By mid-1958, the country was ripe for independence. The colonial administration under Sir Richard Turnbull was sharply aware of the danger of holding back the tide of self rule, having seen the Mau Mau uprising in neighbouring Kenya.

TANU was a mass party that had overwhelming support countrywide. In the August 1960 elections, it won 70 of the 71 seats. Nyerere was appointed Chief Minister. Now the call was for independence before the end of 1961. On 9th December 1961, at the stroke of midnight, the Duke of Edinburgh, on behalf of Queen Elizabeth II, handed over the reins of power to the leaders of the people of Tanganyika in a memorable midnight ceremony. At last, *Uhuru*, independence, had been attained.

Even in the midst of the euphoria, it was realised that Tanganyika's "independence" was mere flag independence. The country was still economically poor and dependent on overseas aid and grants, particularly from Britain, and it still had a great shortage of trained nationals to run the country. When Nyerere resigned as Prime Minister of Tanganyika in January 1962 and left the seat to Rashid Mfaume Kawawa, the founder of the Tanganyika Federation of Labour and then and for many years afterwards, his right hand man, Tanganyika was being prepared for the radical political and economic changes that would put it, and later Tanzania, in the hearts and minds of people the world over. Here was a young and poor country that dared to speak and act openly against colonialism, apartheid, oppression and inequality. Nyerere expressed the mission ahead of the fledgling state with words that ring like the prayer of Saint Francis of Assisi:

> *We, the people of Tanganyika, would like to light a candle on top of Mount Kilimanjaro, which would shine beyond our borders, giving hope where there was despair, love where there was hate and dignity where before there was only humiliation… We cannot, unlike other countries, send rockets to the moon, but we can send rockets of love and hope to our fellow men wherever they may be.*

Nyerere's 'prayer' reflects the incredibly hard choices he and his colleagues in government had to make in determining the destiny of the country. Even before Tanganyika was fully independent, Nyerere had made it clear that independent Tanganyika would not seek membership in a Commonwealth in which South Africa was also a member. In an article published in the *Observer* of 7th March, 1961 under the title 'Commonwealth Choice: South Africa or Us', Nyerere wrote:

> *We believe that South African membership under present conditions makes a mockery of the inter-racial composition of the Commonwealth… We cannot join any 'association of friends' which includes a state deliberately and ruthlessly pursuing a racist policy....*

The effect of this strong and clear message from Tanganyika on Commonwealth leaders can only be imagined, but the courage of such a country as Tanzania in voicing it was monumental. Dr Verwoerd, the South African representative, withdrew his country's application for continuing membership as a republic.

Hand in hand with Tanganyika's commitment to an Africa free of colonialism and oppression, was it's vision of Africa unity. As early as 1961, Nyerere offered to delay the independence of Tanganyika for a whole year if that would bring about the Federation of East Africa. Considering the great fervour and impatience for independence, Nyerere's offer was not idly made.

The January of 1964 was tumultuous for the whole of East Africa. There were mutinies in Tanganyika, Uganda and Kenya. Just before dawn on Sunday, 12th January 1964 a band of forty people, including several retired policemen, stormed and captured Zanzibar's radio station and two police armouries, forcing Sultan Jamshid ibn Abdullah to escape by boat to the mainland and eventually to England. The Revolution was led by Ugandan self-styled Field Marshal John Okello. The massacre that followed is estimated at more than 5,000 dead, most of whom were Arab shopkeepers. Okello then handed over power to a Revolutionary Council under the Afro Shirazi party leader, Sheikh Abeid Karume. On 25th April 1964, Nyerere presented to the Tanganyika National Assembly the proposal for union with Zanzibar, arguing a common language; friendship between Afro Shirazi Party and Tanganyika's TANU; proximity of Zanzibar to the mainland; and above all, Tanganyika's commitment to the cause of African unity. The confederal union that was arrived at the following day was on favourable terms to Zanzibar. That is how Tanzania was born.

In the global arena, Tanzania declared itself to be a non-aligned country, joining other underdeveloped nations which eschewed involvement in the superpower conflict. It was easier said than done and, over a relatively short time, Tanzania found itself more to the East than exactly on the divide between East and West. Three events between 1964 and 1965 can be said to have pushed Tanzania towards the Eastern Bloc: In 1964 the Tanzania Government accused the United States of recruiting mercenaries to overthrow it. This accusation was based on some letters that seemed to implicate the CIA in the alleged plot. Later, they were found to be forgeries, but the rift between the two countries was left unrepaired. In the same year, Tanzania had trouble with the then West Germany, which was the mainland's third biggest aid donor. West Germany had a rigid policy of disassociating itself with countries that had diplomatic ties with East Germany. Because of East Germany's loyalty to Zanzibar, the mainland allowed East Germany to establish a consulate in Dar es Salaam. West Germany withdrew its military aid from Tanzania, and the Tanzanian Government in turn ordered West German technical assistance personnel to leave the country. Then came Rhodesia's Unilateral Declaration of Independence. Tanzania insisted that Britain crush Ian Smith's rebellion, to no avail. Tanzania promptly broke off all diplomatic relations with Britain. In retaliation, Britain stopped a £7.5 million loan it was about to give to Tanzania. In the meantime, China gave Tanzania its first interest free loan and offered to build the 1770 kilometre railway line from Dar es Salaam to Kapiri Mposhi in Zambia.

It cannot be said, however, that Tanzania's friendship with China had a great deal to do with its adoption of Ujamaa which Nyerere, it's founder and guiding spirit, defined simply as 'familyhood'. As early as December, 1962 Nyerere had published a pamphlet entitled *Ujamaa – the Basis of African Socialism*. In it he wrote:

The foundation, and the objective, of African socialism is the extended family. The true African socialist does not look on one class of men as his brethren and another as his natural enemies. He does not form an alliance with the brethren for extermination of the 'non-brethren'. He rather regards all men as his brethren – as members of his ever expanding family. 'Ujamaa', then, or 'familyhood', describes our socialism. It is opposed to capitalism, which seeks to build a happy society on the basis of the exploitation of man by man; and it is equally opposed to doctrinaire socialism which seeks to build it's happy society on a philosophy of inevitable conflict between man and man.

On 5th February 1967, Tanzania formally adopted the socialist path by publication of the Arusha Declaration. The next day President Nyerere announced that all the commercial banks in the country would be nationalised. Then followed the nationalisation of grain milling companies, insurance companies, import-export businesses as well as numerous other manufacturing and processing concerns. Later in 1971 the government nationalised buildings worth 100,000 shillings or more with compensation paid on a sliding scale which came to zero if the nationalised property was more than ten years old.

The timing of the Arusha Declaration and the boas nationalisation were perfect. Nyerere, fondly and reverently called *Mwalimu*, the Teacher, was extolled as the champion for the poor, the workers and peasants who toiled for politicians, civil servants and businessmen who were labelled 'ticks', 'bloodsuckers', 'syphons' and 'parasites'. Long marches in support of the Arusha Declaration sprang up everywhere in the country, and Nyerere himself marched some 220 km in eight days from his village in Mara region to Mwanza town.

The most notable product of the Arusha Declaration was Ujamaa villages. Many of these villages were established at the instance of government or party (TANU) officials. In some cases, like in the infamous *Operation Sogeza* ('Operation Push') force was used to remove families from their traditional homesteads and settle them in 'planned' Ujamaa villages. Little thought was put into the exercise and the people were hardly consulted before a planned Ujamaa village was set up. Listlessness and apathy settled in among most

rural people in mainland Tanzania. Village leadership was often corrupt and bureaucratic. By the end of the 1970s, the average Tanzanian was worse off than he or she was at the beginning of that decade. The 1970s were years when the mistakes committed in the honeymoon years of the 60s were dearly paid for. Onto these troubles were added other problems over which Tanzania had little or no control.

The East African Community collapsed in 1977, requiring the government to provide makeshift arrangements to replace the services hitherto given by the East African Community. In the same year, coffee prices collapsed, leading to tens of millions of dollars of losses in export earnings. Uganda's military dictator, self-styled Field Marshal Idi Amin attacked northern Tanzania in an attempt to turn the people of Uganda's attention from his tyranny to a foreign enemy. First the Tanzanian army repulsed the invaders and, hand in hand with Ugandan opponents in exile, marched to Kampala in April 1979 and forced Amin to flee the country. Having liberated Uganda from Amin's rule, Tanzania continued to support Uganda for a number of years, incurring enormous economic costs. In all, the war cost Tanzania 600 million US dollars including the support of Uganda.

Then came the 1979/80 doubling of oil prices, the 1979 floods, and the 1980 drought. About the same time, the Government of Tanzania quarrelled with the IMF, one of Tanzania's major lenders, over the speed and extent of economic policy changes the country had to take in order to cope with the economic crisis facing it. The IMF was seen to be insensitive to the human and political implications of their recommendations, and Nyerere publicly attacked it, accusing it of wanting to become the 'International Ministry of Finance'. It is remarkable that in the midst of all the political upheavals following the Arusha Declaration, and the financial straits that the country went into in the 1970s and 80s, the people of Tanzania remained united and peaceful and committed, if not at heart at least by rote, to Ujamaa and to their leader, Mwalimu Julius Nyerere.

In 1977, TANU, the political party on mainland Tanzania, and Zanzibar's Afro Shirazi Party merged to form Chama Cha Mapinduzi (CCM) under Nyerere's chairmanship. The parties may have come together, but the union between the mainland and Zanzibar was fraught with dissatisfaction on both sides. Aboud Jumbe, who had succeeded Sheikh Abeid Karume as the Zanzibar leader after the latter was assassinated in 1972, resigned in January 1984 amidst heated debates about the form and the future of the union between Tanganyika and Zanzibar. Ali Hassan Mwinyi succeeded Jumbe and, when Nyerere stepped down as President of Tanzania in 1985, CCM chose Mwinyi as as their candidate for President to succeed *Mwalimu*. He was duly elected by the people.

Nyerere's decision to leave office voluntarily was widely hailed in Tanzania and elsewhere in the world as a unique and wise decision, in contrast to those numerous African dictators who had to be removed from their leadership positions by death or coups d'état. Those who know *Mwalimu* will, however, not fail to notice the perfect timing of his departure. In theory, *Mwalimu* is now an ordinary Tanzanian, without any government position, having retired from Tanzanian politics in May 1991. In reality, Tanzania as well as the Third World looks upon Nyerere as its spokesman whose eloquence and erudition it is hard to gainsay. It is therefore no wonder that the 1986 Non-Aligned Movement summit in Harare appointed him to chair the South Commission that was formally established the following year. The First Report of the Commission that was published in May 1990 advocated mutual co-operation among countries of the South as the only way to gain development and attain bargaining strength against the rich and established countries of the North.

When Ali Hassan Mwinyi took over as President of Tanzania in 1985, he and his government had the herculean task of lifting the country from its economic stagnation. Mwinyi had also to contend with living in the shadow of Nyerere for the entire period of his presidency. Amidst the teetering and falling socialist economies of the world, President Mwinyi gingerly steered the country into economic and polit-

ical liberalisation and out of its socialist path. Mwinyi will be remembered as the long suffering president who brought to Tanzania, and at his expense, freedom of speech and freedom of the press. And although it was Nyerere who gave the nod to acceptance by CCM and the Government of the fact that multi-party democracy was inevitable in Tanzania, it was Mwinyi who appointed a Commission headed by Chief Justice Francis Nyalali to go around the country to seek the opinion of the people on whether the country should adopt multi-partyism. Although the majority of the people interviewed by the Commission preferred a single party 'democracy', it was Mwinyi who gently acted as a mid-wife to multi-party democracy in Tanzania. At the end of his second, and last, term of five years as President of Tanzania, Mwinyi earned the sobriquet "*Mzee Ruksa*", which in Swahili means "the-old-man-who-never-says-no".

The 1995 multi-party presidential and parliamentary elections were contested by a total of thirteen political parties, the main ones being the ruling Chama Cha Mapinduzi (CCM); Civic United Front (CUF); National Convention for Construction and Reform (NCCR-Mageuzi); United Democratic Party (UDP); and Chama Cha Demokrasia na Maendeleo (Chadema). CCM fielded Benjamin William Mkapa, a former journalist, diplomat and Minister; and NCCR-Mageuzi had Augustine Lyatonga Mrema, who had been dismissed from his ministerial post by President Mwinyi and had subsequently resigned his parliamentary seat in protest about corruption and the ruling party's inability to root it out. Mrema was wildly popular among the intelligentsia and the urban working class, but he did not have enough following in rural Tanzania, and

Benjamin Mkapa easily won the presidential election. CCM had a huge majority in parliament.

Mkapa's platform during the 1995 election campaign was his commitment to eliminating corruption root and branch. In December 1996 the Commission that President Mkapa had appointed to inquire into official corruption in Tanzania presented its report. Chaired by Joseph Sinde Warioba, former Prime Minister in Nyerere's Government, the Commission named a number of suspects. It now remains to be seen how the Mkapa Government is going to tackle the rot that is said to have gone to the "highest levels of Government".

It is obvious that prosecuting the individuals named in the report, as demanded by the press and opposition politicians, cannot be enough to get rid of, or even substantially reduce, corruption in Tanzania. Reasons ascribed to this vice have, among others, been poor remuneration to law enforcement officers and government leaders as well as the convergence of official bureaucracy inherited from the Ujamaa days with the incoming liberalization and adoption of a market economy.

Benjamin Mkapa and his Government may deservedly find pride in their success in bringing East African co-operation closer to reality than at any time since the East African Community's collapse in 1977. Tanzania's galloping inflation of the 1980s and early 90s has been arrested to manageable rates, and divestiture of government ownership of parastatal organisations is now well under way. All these seem very ephemeral and Mkapa has the formidable challenge of ministering over and presiding over the country's transition from socialism to capitalism, while at the same time preserving the deep national pride and unity of the Tanzanian people.

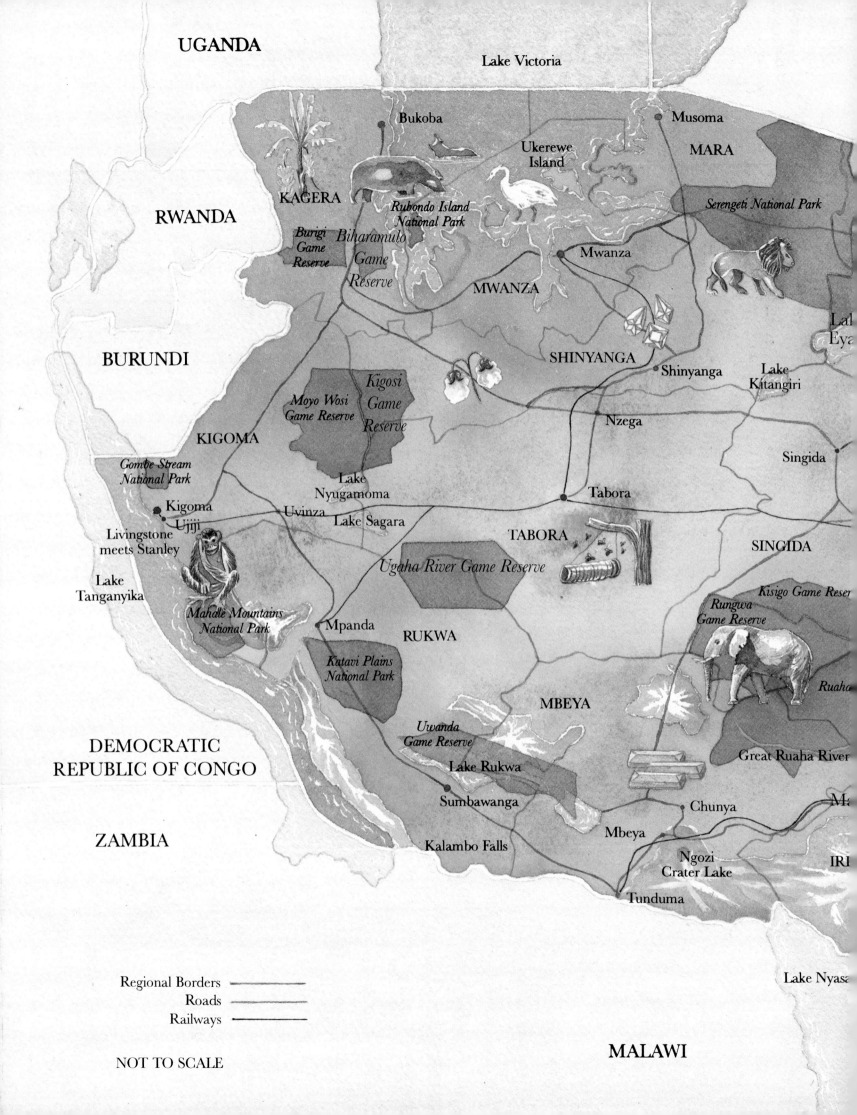

UGANDA

Lake Victoria

Bukoba

Musoma

Ukerewe
Island

MARA

KAGERA

Serengeti National Park

RWANDA

*Rubondo Island
National Park*

*Burigi
Game
Reserve*

*Biharamulo
Game
Reserve*

Mwanza

MWANZA

BURUNDI

SHINYANGA

Shinyanga

Lake
Kitangiri

La
Eya

*Kigosi
Game
Reserve*

*Moyo Wosi
Game Reserve*

Nzega

KIGOMA

Singida

*Gombe Stream
National Park*

Lake
Nyugamoma

Tabora

SINGIDA

Kigoma
Ujiji

Uvinza

Lake Sagara

TABORA

Livingstone
meets Stanley

Ugaha River Game Reserve

Lake
Tanganyika

Mpanda

Kisigo Game Reser

*Rungwa
Game Reserve*

*Mahale Mountains
National Park*

RUKWA

DEMOCRATIC
REPUBLIC OF CONGO

*Katavi Plains
National Park*

Ruaha

MBEYA

*Uwanda
Game Reserve*

Great Ruaha River

Lake Rukwa

ZAMBIA

Sumbawanga

Chunya

Ma

Mbeya

Kalambo Falls

Ngozi
Crater Lake

IRI

Tunduma

Regional Borders

Roads

Railways

Lake Nyasa

NOT TO SCALE

MALAWI

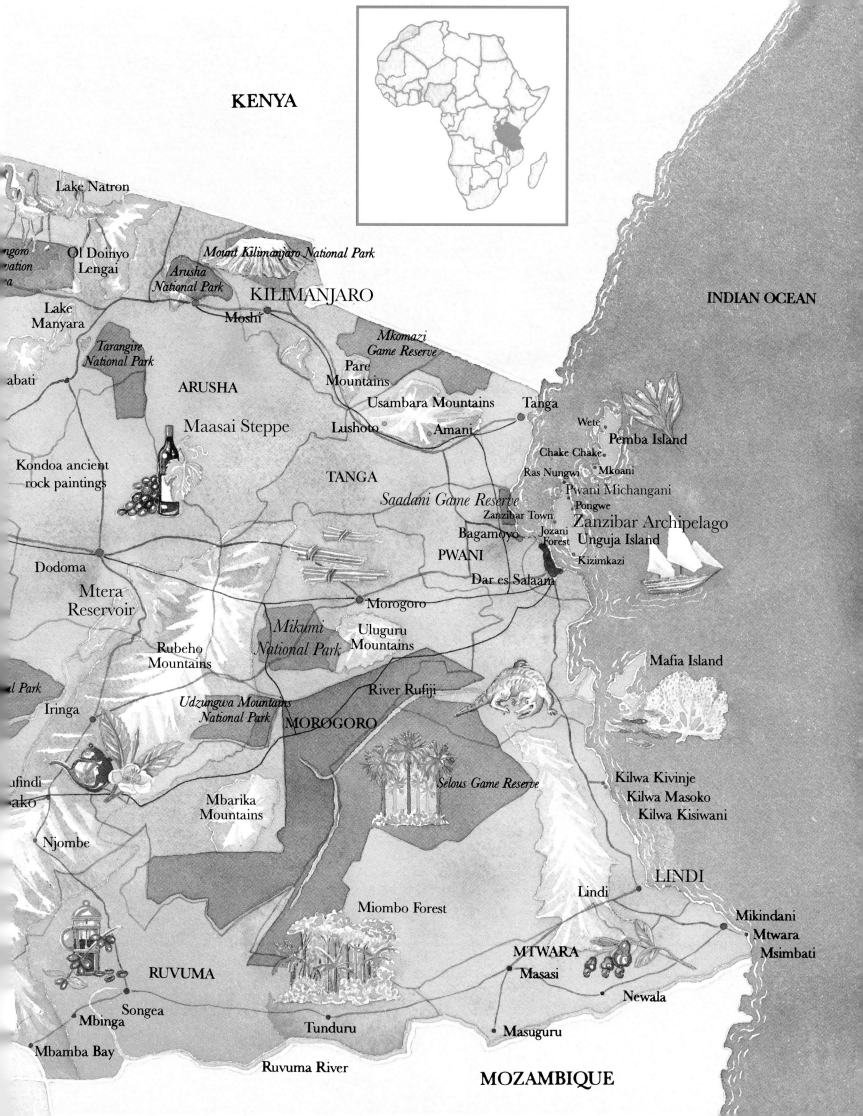

KENYA

INDIAN OCEAN

Lake Natron

Ol Doinyo Lengai

Ngoro
ation
a

Arusha National Park

Mount Kilimanjaro National Park

KILIMANJARO

Lake Manyara

Tarangire National Park

Moshi

abati

Mkomazi Game Reserve

ARUSHA

Pare Mountains

Maasai Steppe

Usambara Mountains

Tanga

Wete

Pemba Island

Lushoto

Amani

Chake Chake

Mkoani

Kondoa ancient rock paintings

TANGA

Ras Nungwi

Pwani Michangani

Pongwe

Saadani Game Reserve

Zanzibar Town

Zanzibar Archipelago

Bagamoyo

Jozani Forest

Unguja Island

Dodoma

PWANI

Kizimkazi

Mtera Reservoir

Dar es Salaam

Mtera Reservoir

Morogoro

Mafia Island

Mikumi National Park

Uluguru Mountains

Rubeho Mountains

River Rufiji

l Park

Udzungwa Mountains National Park

Iringa

MOROGORO

Kilwa Kivinje

ufindi
ako

Mbarika Mountains

Selous Game Reserve

Kilwa Masoko

Kilwa Kisiwani

Njombe

LINDI

Lindi

Miombo Forest

Mikindani

Mtwara

Msimbati

MTWARA

Masasi

RUVUMA

Newala

Mbinga

Songea

Tunduru

Masuguru

Mbamba Bay

Ruvuma River

MOZAMBIQUE

PHOTOGRAPHER'S NOTE

In such a diverse country there are bound to be many conflicting opinions on various subjects. I will mention a couple that spring to mind: Lake Nyasa and Lake Malawi are the same lake and as it is known as both I will refer to it as Lake Nyasa. Also I will call the national language of Tanzania 'Swahili' as opposed to 'Kiswahili' because we are speaking English. Also the names of people groups in Swahili are, for example, Wachagga, but as we are still in English I will refer to them as Chagga. There is a waterfall in Rukwa region on the border with Zambia called Kalambo or Kalamo Falls, I have heard it referred to as both, but for the sake of argument I will refer to it as Kalambo Falls as that seems to be the most commonly used.

Many people ask me about photographing people; I never pay for pictures and will try and spend some time meeting the people I am photographing and then explain what I am doing and always make sure they receive a copy, usually with a Polaroid camera; it would be the same if I was shooting in London, Warsaw or Uganda.

My last thought to you is this: enjoy the book! Just sit back and let me try to show you one of the most amazing countries in the world.

DAR ES SALAAM

*T*he original name for Dar es Salaam was 'Bender-Salaam', which in Arabic means 'Harbour of Peace', and even today poetically inclined Tanzanians call it 'Bandari-ya-Salaam'. The town was built from a harbour on the magnificent shores of Mzizima, which was no more than a small fishing village before 1862. In 1866 Sultan Majid started building his palace which he called 'Dar es Salaam' or 'The Abode of Peace'. Due to its superb harbour and its extensive fresh water supply, Dar es Salaam, as the town was later to be called, attracted much of the business from Kilwa and Bagamoyo. The Germans made it the capital of German East Africa and by 1891 colonial departments had moved in and by 1905 the central railway-line had been started from Dar. This greatly consolidated it as the principal commercial and political centre of the country. When the British took over the administration in 1920, Dar es Salaam remained the capital of Tanganyika with its population growing from a few hundred in 1862 and 128,742 in 1957 to 270,000 in 1967 to approximately 3,000,000 in 1998.

In October 1973, the TANU conference resolved to move the capital of Tanzania from Dar es Salaam to Dodoma. After two or three years of hectic effort, the momentum to move to Dodoma was lost and presently the idea of having Dodoma as capital was seen as impossibly expensive and highly impractical. Dar will thus probably continue to be the de facto capital of Tanzania for a long time to come.

Today, Dar es Salaam buzzes with industrial, commercial, political and diplomatic activity. The port gives sea access to a number of land-locked east and central African countries, as well as for its own import and export market. The TAZARA (Uhuru) Railway to Zambia starts in Dar and there are several fast boat services to Zanzibar, Tanga and Mombasa.

Dar es Salaam has, over the last ten years, greatly improved in appearance. The roads are better surfaced, it is much cleaner and much building has been achieved, including several large hotels. There is a variety of things to do in Dar; from the National Museum and the various art galleries and craft shops and markets to seeing Tingatinga painters at work in Morogoro Stores in Oyster Bay. Alternatively you can go north of Dar a few minutes and relax on the sandy beaches around Kunduchi.

From its Mzizima days, Dar has grown into a pleasant and likeable economic centre without losing its original simplicity and charm. The Zaramo, who are the indigenous people of the region, have now been joined by hundreds of thousands of their fellow Tanzanians from up-country, (whom they used to refer to as *watu wa bara* which is basically translated as 'country bumpkins'). Thus Dar es Salaam has been made into a microcosm of Tanzania, a place where all the people of the country come together to live and work.

1

Dar es Salaam, a city of three million people, with a busy port and centre of commercial activity of Tanzania, can still offer tranquil views over the Indian Ocean.

A few small mangrove trees decorate the ocean near the Selander bridge. Numerous migrating waders use the inter-tidal zone during the spring and autumn migration from Eastern Europe.

There is much building and general infrastructure development throughout Dar.

The Coca Cola factory in Dar. Here the bottles are moving along conveyors past 'sighters', who are checking for cracks, whether they are filled properly and if there are damaged or spoiled bottles.

At the Tingatinga Arts Co-operative Society near Morogoro Stores in Msasani they practise the art of Tingatinga painting. This is an uniquely Tanzanian style of painting started by the late Edward Saidi Tingatinga. He was born in 1932 in the village of Namocheli, Tunduru district in Ruvuma Region. After finishing school, he worked in Tanga and then in 1959 he moved to Dar. In the 60s Tingatinga worked at various jobs in Dar whilst he started to develop his painting. By the start of the 70s his wife, Agata, was selling his pictures at Morogoro Stores, and he was training some of his relatives in his art. Tingatinga then got his first contract with the National Development Corporation. His relatives helped with paintings for the NDC as well as still selling them outside the Morogoro Stores. Very tragically in 1972 Edward Saidi Tingatinga was mistakenly shot and killed by a night-time police patrol.

After his death his memory lived on, and his relatives and friends continued to paint in the style he developed. In 1977 the Tingatinga Partnership was formed and in 1990 the Tingatinga Arts Co-operative Society was established. Today many young people are learning the art of Tingatinga painting at the Society and as the years progress so does the Tingatinga style. As with most art it develops and changes.

The road into Dar from the Selander bridge. After travelling throughout Tanzania on terrible roads you reach Dar and are confronted with this blissful scene of flat smooth tarmac with street lights and traffic lights that work. Long live Dar!

The port in Dar is the largest in the country, handling most of the import and export shipping. It is also the set-off point for all the different types of boat that go to Zanzibar, only about an hour and a quarter away – which is where the boat on the bottom left is off to.

At the fish market in Kivukoni all types of fresh fish are for sale. This one is the Songolo which is the fish you see on the 200 shilling note.

Oyster Bay, just a few kilometres from the centre of town.

Heading north of Dar along the coast you reach an area of beautiful beaches called Kunduchi, which probably got its name from the naked bathers swimming here in the days before swimming clothes were around. Kunduchi literally means 'naked bottoms'.

In the old part of Dar es Salaam you can find lots of beautiful old buildings. This example is on India Street.

Opposite: A large tanker, the sea and palm trees; just a few of the characteristics of my favourite city in East Africa.

TANGA

*T*anga, the place of sails (*tanga* means 'sail' in Swahili) is a quiet, pleasant town with a slightly dilapidated air and many old German colonial buildings lining the main streets. It is a harbour town that once boomed with activity when Tanzania was the world's largest producer of sisal and Tanga was handling most of it for export. Tanga's fertile hinterland of the Usambaras produced, and continues to produce, appreciable quantities of coffee, forest products and tea. A railway-line and a tarmac road link Tanga to these places and to Dar es Salaam. There is likewise a road that goes from Tanga to the harbour city of Mombasa in neighbouring Kenya.

Tanga saw the opening of the First World War conflict in German East Africa when the British attacked the town in November 1914 from the sea and met with stiff resistance from the Germans and, fortuitously for the Germans, a huge swarm of bees. The attack was not particularly successful.

The Tanga region has much to offer the visitor: The Amboni caves near Tanga town are the most extensive limestone caves in the whole of East Africa, and definitely worth exploring. Pangani town, much older than Tanga and very picturesque, has the best beaches in the whole region and has changed very little over the last one hundred years. As one travels westwards inland, the Usambara mountains roll for miles, verdant and cool. The Germans called this part of the country Wilhelmstal and loved it more than any other in German East Africa. They established the Amani agricultural and medical research centre which still exists today. They also built the Bumbuli Hospital and the Vuga Press which continues to publish Christian tracts and books. Ornithologists will love the Usambara mountains for its vast variety of birds. Walking up and across these mountains is rewarding to the enthusiast and kind to the environment.

The lowlands under the Usambaras are fertile farmlands well watered by the Pangani river. Rice, maize, beans and citrus fruit grow in great abundance. The rest of the drier plains are taken up by vast tracts of sisal plantations that suffered from the fall in sisal prices in the 1970s and 80s and are now, with recovering sisal prices, slowly picking up again and getting privatised.

Tanga is the land of, among others, the Zigua, Bondei, Sambaa and Digo people. As you can tell from the name of the highlands, the Sambaa people live in the Usambara mountains, the Bondei people (*bonde* is 'valley' in Swahili) live in the lowlands and are closely associated with the Zingua. The Digo live on the coast.

Market Street in Tanga town shows a definite colonial influence in some of its exotic architecture.

Tanga Port is the main export point for the north and western regions of Tanzania. These containers could be filled with coffee, seed beans or other commodities.

In the First World War a German, General Paul von Lettow-Vorbeck, caused the Allies great trouble in Tanganyika. He was so brilliant that he was never actually beaten and at the end of the war surrendered honourably (see Introduction). General von Lettow-Vorbeck used Tanganyikan men called Askaris in his army. Today there is only one of Vorbeck's Askaris, Saidi Musa, still alive and he is here talking to Jane Tamé. She is an Englishwoman who, for the last 11 years, has been paying the remaining Askaris their pensions on behalf of the German Government. When she started doing this in 1987 there were 8 Askaris left, now there is only one. History rarely shows itself so graphically.

The Amboni Caves, just outside Tanga. These
are the most extensive limestone caves in East
Africa and still hold a certain superstitious grip
on the local people. They believe there is a god
who heals, living in the caves. As you walk round
you can occasionally see candles and small offer-
ings left for this god.

Pangani town is just over 50 kilometres from Tanga along the coast. It is a fairly popular place to visit because of some nice beaches and good fishing. The town is on the north bank of the River Pangani and as Philip Briggs writes in his *Guide to Tanzania*, "...Pangani is relaxed and sleepy, and like so many coastal towns, it does not seem to belong to the 20th century."

One feature of the area is that there is a large amount of betel or areca-nut produced here. This is a sweet palm nut very popular among the Asian community for eating as a sweet. Leonard Mkavila shows me how the outer shell comes off to reveal the actual nut, seen in the bag. He said they were very tasty; I took his word for it.

Amani is a small village in the East Usambara Mountains. In 1902 the Germans established an agricultural research station here and they also set aside the surrounding land as a botanical garden. Much of the garden is still here and makes the area very beautiful. The East Usambaras are mainly forest reserves so there are few people living there, compared with the West Usambaras which have a considerable population.

Near Amani is the tea estate of the East Usambara Tea Company. Tea has been farmed in these highlands for many years and is exported around the world, particuarly to Pakistan and the UK, usually after auction in Mombasa, Kenya.

The West Usambaras are well populated and farmed, as the area is very fertile and accessible. Crops can be taken away for sale in Dar or other closer towns.

Coffee is also grown in the Usambaras. The type grown is arabica due to the high altitude of the mountains. Here the people are pulping the coffee with a hand pulper. This removes the fleshy parts and red skin of the ripe cherry. The beans are then washed, fermented over one or two days, washed again and dried in the sun for about ten days.

The Usambara Mountains as seen from the road to Dar es Salaam on the south-west side of the mountains.

KILIMANJARO

*L*egend has it that Mount Kilimanjaro and its environs were part of British East Africa, and one day in 1886 Queen Victoria decided to give it to her cousin, the German Emperor, Wilhelm. Thus the border was apparently shifted and Kilimanjaro became part of German East Africa. However, in 1996 one hundred and ten years on, a former German Ambassador to Tanzania, Dr. Heinz Sneppen, has disputed this story arguing that Wilhelm was not the Queen's cousin but her grandson and nor was Wilhelm the German Emperor at the time. He also claims that it would have been highly unlikely for her to have given him anything, considering she thought he was a "hot-headed, wrong-headed, conceited young man devoid of all feelings". Whatever happened in those convoluted negotiations and haggling in the scramble for Africa, Kilimanjaro is in Tanzania.

The regional capital, Moshi, is named after the former chiefdom of Mochi, in whose lowland the town lies. The original Moshi or Old Moshi is higher up the mountain and until the railway-line reached the present Moshi in 1911 and a station built, the headquarters of the German administrative district of Moshi was there. Today's Moshi was originally called "Shashioni", a corruption of the word "station", due to the railway station.

Kilimanjaro is a region of two main ethnic groups; the Chagga people who live on and around Mount Kilimanjaro and the Pare who live in the Pare Mountains. The main agricultural activity in the region is coffee and some of the finest Arabica in Tanzania comes from the slopes of Kilimanjaro. The coffee grown here is the livelihoods for hundreds of thousands of people.

The geography of the region is quite remarkable; starting at Mount Kilimanjaro you move down the slopes to the flat plains south of the mountains then move east and you encounter the Pare Mountains, a range of mountains highly populated on their north side but not so on their south side.

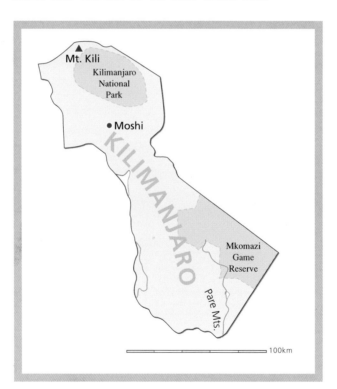

Behind these mountains lies Mkomazi Game Reserve, a beautiful reserve with one of its special features being the protection of endangered species. When you look west from the Pare Mountains you look over what seems to be endless flat plains, the Maasai Steppe. This is an everlasting wilderness where the Maasai live, among other places. The region is as diverse as any in the country, in landscape, people and culture, most of which you should try to discover yourself.

Moshi, the capital of the region, nestles in the shadow of Mount Kilimanjaro.

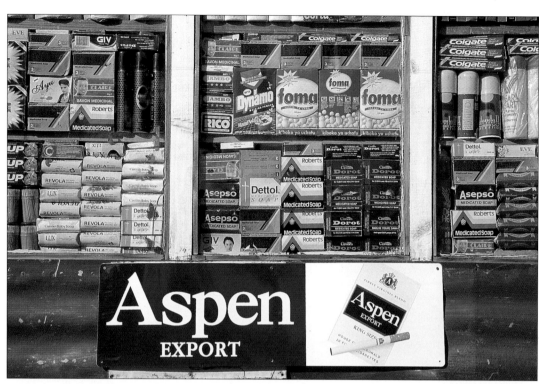

A portable shop sells, as usual, a wide range of goods.

Moshi has rail links to Arusha, Tanga, Dar es Salaam and into Kenya: all vital for the area's agricultural exports. The old East African Railway left a few of its steam engines and carriages around the edges of the station.

This monument on the outside of Moshi town is to commemorate the Tanzanians who died in the war in Kagera region against Idi Amin of Uganda in 1978. The road to Dar goes off into the distance.

All over the region the co-operative societies and the large coffee companies based in Moshi have coffee-buying stations in the rural areas. This is the place where the farmer comes to sell his coffee to the people who offer him the best deal. The gentleman on the left appears to be checking today's price, which according to the middle sign is 800 shillings per kilo.

In Moshi town Milcafe Limited, amongst others, operates a coffee export factory. Here the sacks are being prepared with the company logo and details of the coffee that they will contain.

Inside the factory the coffee goes through various stages of cleaning and grading. This is the 'gravity separator' or 'densimetric table' which processes each grade of coffee individually in order to separate the lighter beans from the solid beans.

The graded coffee is then auctioned in Moshi. After auction the buyer often has the coffee hand-picked so that it is in top condition for export.

The hand-picked coffee is then re-bulked to ensure an even quality. Here the coffee is being unloaded from the bulking machine and bagged. The worker will open the chute to let 60 kilos of coffee into the bag. From here the coffee will be exported all over the world.

Near the village of Usangi in the North Pare Mountains this man is building a maize store. The work started a week ago and he told us he hoped to finish in a couple of days. Fast work.

Kurwa is 14 years old and started to learn how to make clay pots this year. While we were visiting him, he made one extremely quickly with highly dexterous fingers. The pots are mainly used for cooking. After turning them on the wheel, they are dried for two weeks and then baked under burning grass for an hour and a half. They are sold through a local women's group.

25

The North Pare Mountains are quite densely populated and farming is extensive. Lake Jipe in the distance is in fact half in Kenya on the north-east side of the North Pare Mountains.

Kilimanjaro National Park

Kilimanjaro, standing on Tanzania's northern boundary, is the highest mountain in the African continent. Actually formed from two extinct and one dormant volcanoes, its loftiest peak reaches 19,340ft (5895m).

Although this park is now one of the most popular in Tanzania, the mountain's past remains rather mysterious, as do the origins of its name. While its two main peaks have been long familiar to the African eye, its history is documented somewhat haphazardly. Strangely, it receives only one mention from the ancient traders whose route followed the east African coast. However, Kilimanjaro was lifted out of this global obscurity by the accounts and records of 19th-century missionaries and explorers, who drew international attention to the wonders of the African continent.

The Kilimanjaro National Park of today contains some of the most breathtakingly beautiful scenery in Tanzania. Perhaps its greatest strength is the variety of its landscapes, which range from rain forest through moorland to desert and, finally, to snow-covered peaks. Of course, such a varying landscape makes for a highly varied climate; weather conditions on Kilimanjaro range from extremely warm and dry on the lower plains to consistently below freezing on the summit. For hikers, there are several marked routes up the mountain, none of which should take more than six days to complete. Each of these routes has its own appeal, but the most beautiful is probably the Machame route which meanders gently through forestry before broadening to allow stunning views of the Shira Plateau.

Indeed, it is scenery such as this which makes Kilimanjaro such an extraordinary place, worth visiting even if you are not planning a full ascent. The forest zone, the most verdant on the mountain, boasts a fascinating and abundant selection of plants, trees and flowers. Less easy to come by is the resident wildlife; although most of the animals on Kilimanjaro live in the forest, they are not always readily visible. If you can catch a glimpse of the black and white colobus monkeys, leaping between the trees, then you will have done well.

The contrast between the forestry and the highland desert could hardly be greater, yet the bleak landscape of the latter is equally spectacular. Although little wildlife can survive at this altitude, the daylight views of the mountain's glaciers and dykes and the views of the night sky are well worth the long trek.

"The ethereal peak of Mount Kilimanjaro rises out of the dawn mists."
Even this illiterate photographer is stunned into performing great feats of literary brilliance
by the awesomeness of the highest free-standing mountain in the world.

The mountain has a wide range of wildlife; from mammals and birds to a plethora of small reptiles and insects. Due to the huge numbers of people who climb 'Kili' you are lucky to see any of these. We were very fortunate to see a large family of Blue or Syke's monkeys, *Cercopithecus mitis*, close to Mandara Hut.

Mandara Hut: on 'Kili' there are various routes you can take and on most of these routes the National Parks provide accommodation and eating places. The most popular route is the Marangu route, alternatively known as the Coca Cola route, due to being the easiest way up. Mandara Hut at 2750m is the first hut you reach on the Marangu route after a fairly short and pleasant walk up through the forest. The hut is named after a Chagga chief from the late nineteenth century called Rindi of Moshi, who was also called Mandara.

A chameleon diversifies our game viewing on the mountains on the way up to Horombo Hut from Mandara Hut.

The heath and moorland zone is characterised by a more open landscape littered with lobelia, *Lobelia deckenii*, and tree groundsels, *Senecio kilimanjarica*, as well as a few bogs, just to keep you alert.

Left: Kilimanjaro has a broad range of plant life all the way up the mountain, even to the high areas. This pink everlasting daisy, *Compositae*, is one of the many flowers you can see in the heath and moorland zone between 3000 and 4000m.

The views from Horombo Hut at 3720m are quite spectacular. Here you can see the Pare Mountains in the distance and a porter arriving at the hut bearing someone's food. Horombo Hut was named after the Chagga chief, Horombo, of the early nineteenth century who was assasinated by the Maasai.

The views of the summit of 'Kili' from Horombo Hut are amazing. The summit has had a recent snowfall covering most of it in a stunning white blanket. One sadness of looking at the ice cap these days is the dramatic way it is receding. If you ask anyone who had seen the ice cap some years ago they will undoubtedly confirm that it has got smaller. One explanation is that the deforestation in the area has reduced the cloud cover which used to protect the ice cap from the sun for most of the day. The times change, countries develop all over the world, but at what cost? At whose expense? The environment often seems to suffer.

From Horombo Hut to the last hut, Kibo Hut, at 4750m (there seem to be a few differing opinions on the actual altitude of Kibo so I will go with the sign on the door of the hut) you can take two routes: one via Mawenzi peak and the other more direct and straight forward. The porters and guides who go with you up the mountain are an exceptional bunch of people, their strength and perseverance quite unmatched.

At Horombo Hut you have an option of acclimatising for an extra day, going on a short walk around the area. You can also get great views of Mawenzi peak, 5149m, seen here. To climb to the top of Mawenzi, you need to be an experienced climber with all the right equipment and of course great skill, determination and immense courage. We would have done it, of course, but by some strange coincindence had left our equipment behind…

As you prepare to walk up to Kibo your nerves are beginning to tingle with the notion of reaching the peak or not; failure or success. Kibo is only the set-off point for the summit anyway. The reason you are there is to reach the highest point in Africa – to achieve. I am sure that this chap legging it in the wrong direction shows what many of us have felt: let me go now rather than not making it later. Or, of course, I could be the only person who has felt like that…

From the Saddle approaching Kibo Hut you can get great views of Mawenzi peak. We saw Mawenzi after a recent snowfall, giving it this strange alpine volcanic image.

Protas Mtui, our legend of a mountain guide, puts a brave face on the chilly weather at the top. Protas spends some of the year as a mountain guide and the rest of the time he looks after his farm on the mountainside. He has climbed to the peak over a hundred times and, luckily for us (unsurprisingly really), he could find his way back from Uhuru Peak in a snow storm.

Climbing to the top of Mount Kilimanjaro is by no means a picnic. The first few days have been comfortable walks and it is from Kibo Hut that all the fun stops and the agony begins. From Kibo Hut you will climb about 1145m in about 5 or 6 hours in the dark. It is a slow process, one foot after another, rest, keep going on and on until, eventually, about 4 years later, you reach Gillman's Point, and then it is another 2 hours or 3 weeks, depending on your point of view, to reach Uhuru peak, 5895m. We were especially fortunate to be escorted up to the peak by a snow blizzard, because we needed the extra challenge – like a hole in the head. Here you can see eminent London barrister Tom Cleeve veritably charging up the mountain behind Protas Mtui, our guide. We are, at this point, shortly to arrive at Gillman's Point.

Reaching Uhuru has to be one of my most exhilarating feelings of athletic achievement. Fair enough, that's not too difficult of course – however it felt good. It was very cold and we couldn't see very far, but we could all feel the essence of the mountain; it is genuinely a high mountain. I think, because so many people go up it, the awesomeness can be forgotten and the danger overlooked. On the top, at 6.20am, it had been a challenge to climb and although we weren't offered the amazing views many people experience, we were shown another side to the mountain, the snowy side!

This picture shows Fred Ploner, a climber from Italy, about to write his name in the register which stays permanently at the top. From here we returned to Kibo Hut for a brief rest and then on to Horombo Hut. In Kibo Hut there is a visitors book for your comments on descending from the peak. Tom Cleeve wrote the following: "Probably the stupidest thing I've ever done".

M k o m a z i   G a m e   R e s e r v e

Mkomazi Game reserve is a magnificent 3500 sq km reserve in northern Tanzania. It is a spectacular wilderness. Within sight to the north-west is Mount Kilimanjaro, Africa's highest summit. To the south, the Pare and Usambara Mountains form a dramatic backdrop, and to the north, Kenya's vast Tsavo National Park shares a common boundary with Mkomazi, making common ground for migratory herds of elephant, oryx and zebra during the wet season. Together with Tsavo it forms one of the largest and most important ecosystems on earth

Mkomazi was gazetted by the Government of Tanzania in 1951, but never attracted the financial support for the better known wildlife strongholds such as the Serengeti and Ngorogoro. By 1988 it was in steep decline, representing a classic example of degradation from overgrazing, burning, hunting and poaching. In 1988 the Government of Tanzania decided to re-examine its status, with a view to ensuring the complete rehabilitation of this vast area. The Government invited the George Adamson Wildlife Preservation Trust to help them undertake a programme of habitat restoration and endangered species programmes for the African hunting dog and the black rhino.

The African hunting dog are a vanishing species. Mysterious, elusive, enigmatic, they are the restless corsairs of the African plains. They possess no territories. Only when the bitches whelp does the pack settle down for a few months until the pups are old enough to accompany them on their marathon journeys. The African hunting dogs are the wolves of Africa. Their heads are broad, their muzzles short. There is strength in the muscular neck, stamina in the deep chest, tenacity and endurance in their long, slim legs. They seldom raise their hunting pace above 30 miles an hour but can maintain a steady speed for miles, wearing down their prey in a remorseless and single-minded chase to the death. For years they were despised as vermin, shot, poisoned by farmers, hunters, pastoralists and game wardens alike. They have become fugitives, a vanishing breed. All over Africa their history has been one of unremitting persecution. Only when more enlightened attitudes began to prevail were they seen in their own true light – not as indiscriminate butchers, but as highly intelligent social animals. The aim of the George Adamson Wildlife Preservation Trust's programme is to establish a breeding base to translocate them back to areas where they will have the best chance of success.

The black rhino has come dangerously close to the end of the trail. Today, there are fewer than 3000 left and every survivor lives with a price on its head. The rhino horn is used for dagger handles in the Yemen and as an analgesic in Asia, where it is worth more than twice its weight in gold. Today, wildlife managers are moving rhinos around like threatened pieces in a chess game. Mkomazi is home to the first rhino sanctuary in Tanzania, constructed and funded by the George Adamson Wildlife Preservation Trust. Heavily guarded sanctuaries are now essential for the survival of the species.

The rebuilding of Mkomazi Game Reserve, the rehabilitation of its wildlife including the endangered species programmes and projects in the community, are an attempt to re-establish complete ecosystems, positively reversing the damage that has been done. It is essential that we should now master the techniques of revival and renewal, so that ecosystems become self sustaining. That process is the driving force behind the Mkomazi Project. The Trusts believe it to be one of the most important projects in Africa today.

The George Adamson Wildlife Preservation Trust.

39

In the dry season the game moves into Kenya in search of better food and the area becomes arid. The reserve is dominated by flat plains interspersed with small and not so small hills.

Photo: Frank Teulling

This is the armed patrol walking the 32 km long perimeter fence of the Rhino sanctuary. It is a maximum security area and is guarded by armed patrols on foot and in Landrovers. The fence is fully electrified, using 12,000 poles and 500 km of wire, and every stretch is continually watched from observation hills.

This is Rose, a female black rhino. She arrived at the Mkomazi sanctuary by plane with three others on 4th November 1997 from the Addo Elephant park in South Africa.

Photo: Frank Teulling

The African wild dog or hunting dog, *Lycaon pictus*, which means 'painted wolf', is an apt description as the white patches on each dog are unique. Some time ago wild dogs were virtually obliterated from the Serengeti by disease which is why there is much medical research done on these dogs here, to try and assess their reactions to certain inoculations. There are also DNA studies to show their biodiversity. Wild dogs are still found in low densities in large tracts of land in the woodland of southern Tanzania.

The man who knows the wild dogs of Mkomazi better than anyone is Sengito. He was part of the team which rescued the puppies from the Maasai Steppe when they were about 3-4 weeks old. If the pups had been left, it is more than likely that they would have been killed as vermin, a tragedy for one of Africa's most amazing creatures. He now looks after three *bomas* of wild dogs full-time, helping with the medical research as well as all the feeding and other jobs.

These wild dogs are, after the cheetah, the most efficient carnivorous hunters in
Africa. They hunt in packs and are able to maintain speeds of 56kph (35mph)
for several kilometres and at least 48kph up to 5 kilometres. These speeds are
slightly lower than a gazelle's top speed but it is their impressive endurance
which means they can run most game to exhaustion. (Information thanks to
Richard Despard Estes' *The Behaviour Guide To African Mammals, p.415.*)

The wild dog is an immensely sociable creature. They have a convoluted greeting process
when they wake up and in the evening. After a successful hunt, almost all of the pack will
return to the den and very unselfishly regurgitate food for the Alpha female and her puppies.
In case you hadn't guessed, these wonderful creatures are my favourite African animals.

A rock hyrax, *Procavia johnstoni*, poised ready for flight. It is said they are the closest living relative to the elephant – unsure about this as they come from from a different Order. However they do have "...clawless feet not unlike an elephant's..." (Estes. p.251)

Meet Nina, a 28-year-old female African Elephant, who was recently moved from a zoo-type place in Arusha to the reserve. She now enjoys the full freedom of reserve life and looks forward, I'm sure, to meeting the other elephants of the reserve. Short tusks are common among captive (or ex-captive) elephants because they never have the opportunity to use them in the same way as wild elephants.

ARUSHA

*A*rusha region holds a great diversity of peoples. It is the home of the Maasai as well as the Meru, Arusha, Iraqw, Tatoga, Sandawe and Hadza. The Maasai, one of the strongest Nilotic groups in east Africa, who are well known for their warrior-like ways, are pastoralists and cattle are intrinsic in their society. The Meru come from the mountain and the Arusha have much in common with the Maasai except the Arusha have turned to agriculture as opposed to cattle. The Iraqw have Cushitic origins from Ethiopia and beyond the Red Sea – the language is heavily laced with Arabic. The Tatoga are another Nilotic group less prolific than the Maasai, while the Sandawe are the remaining Khoisan speakers left in east Africa, apart from the few Hadza left around Lake Eyasi. The Hadza are the last hunter-gatherers in east Africa and their lives are certainly under pressure. (See Singida region.) It is impossible to be exact when talking geography and peoples but these groups are all in Arusha region as well as in the surrounding regions too.

Arusha is a busy, modern town, nestling in the shadow of Mount Meru and plays host to the Commission on East African Co-operation and the Arusha International Conference Centre, which was once the home of the Organisation for East African Unity. The town could be referred to as the heart of the country's tourism industry, probably due to the proximity of Arusha to the Northern Safari circuit, which includes Tarangire National Park Lake Manyara National Park and the Ngorongoro Conservation Area, all within the Arusha

region; as well as the Serengeti National Park which is in Mara and Shinyanga regions.

Arusha region also features the active volcano that the Maasai call Ol'Doinyo Lengai ('Mountain of God') and Lake Natron, a soda or alkaline lake both in the northern reaches of the region. Lake Eyasi, in the southern part of the region, is another soda lake around which fertile land irrigated by many natural springs supports the intensive cultivation of onions.

Arabica coffee is grown in a number of large plantations and also in small holdings owned by families of the Arusha and Meru

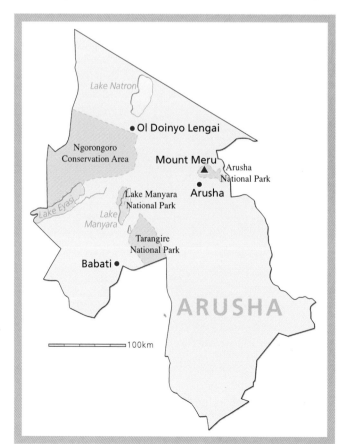

people. Tanzanite, a semi-precious gemstone, is mined in areas around the Blue Mountain in the south-east of Arusha and good quality stones can be purchased from the many gemstone shops in Arusha. The South Maasai Steppe in the south of Arusha region stretches as far as the eye can see, without many permanent habitations and is the grazing ground for the thousands of Maasai cattle.

To the north, Arusha shares a border with Kenya. Namanga, the border town, is quickly growing from a village to a full-sized town as business and travel between Tanzania and Kenya increases in volume. From Namanga, a good tarmac road goes to Arusha and out of the country to Nairobi.

The Arusha International Conference Centre (AICC), located in the heart of Arusha town, is very much a sign of the way Arusha developed from a small town of 30,000 in the early sixties into the international centre that it is today. The building was completed in 1977 and was at that time the headquarters of the East African Community. When the EAC broke up, the building became the AICC and now offers conference facilities as well as offices.

One of the features of Arusha's main street is its eating places. Here is one small example of the quality restaurants you find here.

The clocktower roundabout in the centre of Arusha town.

Arusha is also a major coffee growing area. Here at the Burka Coffee Estate, arabica coffee is grown. There are several other privately owned estates in and around Arusha, including Selian, Mringa and Monduli.

A group of Tanzanite miners in Mererani in the Blue Mountains, behind Kilimanjaro
International Airport. Tanzanite is a semi-precious stone found only in Tanzania and, within
Tanzania, only in a couple of places. There are about 40 small mines in this area, not all of
which are working. Graphite is the other mineral mined on a large scale in the area.

The Maasai people definitely know how to dance and to celebrate certain key occasions. After the circumcision of a group of boys there is much rejoicing as all the boys who were circumcised are qualified to be *Moran* or warriors. The celebrations and dancing continue for the day and night following the ceremony.

For certain occasions, the Maasai will drink the blood of the cow, either on its own or mixed with milk. The blood is taken from the cow by punching the prominent jugular vein with an arrow with a small metal point on a thick end. This means that the vein will get a small hole punched into it which heals more easily than cutting it with a knife. Here you can see the cow, with the leather thong around its neck to exaggerate the jugular vein, being held. The arrow is about to be let loose on the unsuspecting vein.

These lads have recently been circumcised and are preparing to become *Moran*. The white paint on the faces and the ostrich feathers on the head show the significance of their position. The circumcision ceremony takes place between June and December, just after the long rains, so the cows are healthy and able to produce good milk and oil. The milk is used as ceremonial cleaning after the actual operation and pure oil is what the boys consume immediately after the operation, usually between three and five litres.

Blood is collected in a traditional gourd, which is made from the fruit of a pumpkin-like plant. The cow will recover almost immediately. It was kindly donating a bit of blood, nothing more.

The Maasai women have different coloured cloaks according to their matrimonial status. The married women who have borne children have the purple cloaks; the married women without children wear blue; and the unmarried women and girls wear maroon. The heads are shaved and ochre is put on their faces for these special occasions. The men also shave their heads in certain designs and put ochre on their faces.

The Maasai are a warm and welcoming group of people and they made my stay with them greatly enjoyable.

Lake Eyasi is a large soda lake found on the edge of the Rift Valley. Most of the year it is fairly dry and only occasionally during the rains will it fill with water and even then it is not very deep. However, although water doesn't show, there is no lack of mud underneath the dry crust. This could get the unwary traveller well and truly stuck.

This is Emmanuel Mattya who is uprooting onion shoots for replanting. At this stage the onions are about two weeks old. Three months after the replanting the onions will be ready to harvest.

Near Lake Eyasi is a village called Mang'ola. The village is small and not particularly remarkable, except for two things: firstly, it is situated next to Lake Eyasi, an enormous dry soda lake and secondly, it is the foremost producer of onions in the whole of Tanzania. The entire region is extraordinary. There is an area called Quan'dend, surrounded by semi-arid desert, which is irrigated by many natural springs. On this massively fertile plain, onions are farmed on a huge scale. Most of the farms are fairly small, but there are thousands of them. Mang'ola, it is said, sells approximately 600 bags of onions a day! Each bag weighs about 100 kilos. Buyers come here from all over Tanzania and even from Nairobi, Kenya, to get their onions.

Lake Natron, also on the edge of the Rift Valley, leading to the Kenya border, is a soda (i.e. Sodium carbonate) lake. The area immediately around the lake has soda about one or two metres below the surface. It is excavated and left in piles like these. The Maasai have various uses for soda; after dissolving it in boiling water it is used for washing clothes (problem with this is that it rots the clothes very quickly). It is also used in cooking.

Lesser flamingoes *Phoenicopterus minor* are fairly abundant in such areas as soda lakes through-out East Africa. Lake Natron is noted as being a particular breeding site for them.

It is often quite difficult to get close to the flamingoes on Lake Natron. In a place like this, you are likely to get totally and utterly stuck in your vehicle because what looks like dry and hard ground is in fact a trick of Mother Nature to try to lure unsuspecting vehicles into her cunning trap. We ventured as close as possible and then noticed ahead vehicle tracks which ended in two very large holes. As that unlucky car had obviously got terribly bogged down, we decided to go the rest of the way on foot, which is when the fun really started. We survived, just.

Ol Doinyo Lengai, the Mountain of God. An active volcano which last erupted in 1983 obliterating the surrounding vegetation. It has returned but not to any great extent and no-one is sure when the volcano might erupt again.

Arusha National Park

Situated on the eastern edge of the Great Rift Valley, Arusha is among the smallest of Tanzania's eleven National Parks, extending to a mere 137sq km. However, the parkland, located in a very populous area of Tanzania, encompasses some stunningly varied wildlife and landscapes, and includes areas where the Maasai people once lived. The park can be divided into three areas, each with a specific character of its own: the Ngurdoto Crater, the Momela Lakes, sustained by underground streams, and Mount Meru, a dormant volcano, from whose summit Kilimanjaro can be seen in all its glory.

The Ngurdoto Crater, created by the activities of the now extinct Ngurdoto volcano, and measuring a full three kilometres across, is an extraordinary sight. It can be best viewed from one of the many observation points situated around its rim. In addition, the crater affords excellent opportunities for viewing the surrounding countryside. Leitong, the crater's highest point, offers clear views of the Momela Lakes and on a fine day, Kilimanjaro can be seen from Mikindu Point.

Ngurdoto Forest, situated in the south-eastern corner of the park, is notable for the variety of its plant and wildlife and is well worth a visit. Among the most striking, although not the most even-tempered, of the animals is the Olive baboon. Living in large troops, the antics of these mammals and their offspring are wonderful to watch. As the forest begins to thin out north of Ngurdoto, small groups of African elephants can sometimes be seen during the day and at night the chilling cry of the Spotted hyena is heard.

Situated in the north-eastern corner of the Arusha park are the beautiful Momela Lakes. Since these bodies of water each nourish different types of algae, all vary slightly in colour and are home to widely varying types of bird and plant life. The most visually striking of the birds that live around the lakes is,

of course, the flamingo, whose pink plumage and awkward gait are familiar yet compelling. The lakes also play host to cumbersome hippopotami, whose apparent placidity belies a sometimes ferocious temper.

Last but not least, Mount Meru, in the west of the park, boasts a great variety of hills, forests and open plains. Groups of grazing buffaloes can often be glimpsed in forest glades, above which tawny eagles are seen in flight. On emerging from the forest, however, one is confronted by the bleak beauty of the Meru Crater and one of the tallest cliff faces in the world. This shift in the nature of the landscape is sudden and startling, yet epitomises the dramatic and constantly surprising nature of Tanzania's parkland.

An inquisitive Maasai giraffe pokes his head up above the vegetation.

A herd of Common waterbuck, *Kobus ellipsiprymnus*. There are two types of waterbuck, the Common waterbuck and the Defassa waterbuck. The Common have white hoops like these on their rumps and the Defassa has a white patch on the rump.

Tululusia River, which flows over the hill of the same name, comes flying down a waterfall you can see on the walk up Mount Meru.

Kirk's Dik-dik, *Madoqua kirkii*, one of the dwarf antelopes. A family-minded creature, they mate with one partner for life.

A herd of Maasai giraffe drinking from one of the larger Momela lakes in the north-east of the park.

By climbing Mount Meru you have the opportunity to walk through the park amidst any wildlife you can find. Alternatively you can drive to the first hut. Strangely I chose to walk, the chance to be with animals without the safety of a car being too good to miss. This is my guide, Freddy Joshua Swai, carefully watching a few buffaloes on the right.

Opposite: The views as you climb Meru are quite extraordinary, especially of its neighbour Kilimanjaro and the plains in front of it.

From the peak of Little Meru, you can see Mount Meru, the crater, the ash cone and the two Saddle huts at 3500m. Little Meru reaches 3820m and is a quick walk up from Saddle Hut.

The peak of Mount Meru is at 4566m and, like Kilimanjaro, to walk to the summit you set off in the middle of the night – highly unsociable. The route takes you along the ridge all the way to the top, the descent is often shrouded in mist. You can make out Freddy in his white balaclava in the middle.

The full view of Meru and the ash cone from the first hut, Miriakamba Hut at 2500m. The ash cone has been built up over the last 250,000 years since the first major eruption, by subsequent volcanic activity.

Tarangire National Park

Tarangire seemed to be a "forgotten paradise". Passing the entrance gate at the headquarters, the visitor is invited to enjoy the impressive beauty of huge Baobab trees and old Acacia trees. As if time stood still, this landscape lets you imagine how mighty and timeless nature can be.

The park's main feature is the Tarangire river which flows like a live wire from the south to the north of the park and into Lake Burungi. A drive through the park offers you magnificent landscapes: Baobab trees, grasslands, beautiful Acacia parkland, Doum palms and black cotton grassland which forms a huge swamp during the rainy season in April and May.

The drive along the river offers good big-game contact since most of the mammals have to come down to the river to drink. Especially by October/November, numerous zebras and wildebeests have arrived in great numbers and offer one of the most impressive game viewing opportunities. But even during the rest of the season, bird life is abundant and many elephants remain in the park circling its northern or southern part.

Visitors who stay a few days will soon be caught by the rhythm of the daily life cycle: the calls of doves and other birds at sunrise; the amazing colours with which the early sunlight paints the landscapes; during the late morning hours the migration of mammals down to the river (watch how carefully the leading zebra guides its thirsty group to the river to drink). During the heat of the day, elephants gather in the shade of trees flapping their ears to keep cool but as late afternoon brings back the beautiful light, most of the animals leave the river area. At night you can hear a lion's roar, a hyena's 'laugh' or the screams of baboons fighting for their sleeping places in the trees, adding to the sounds of the insects and other voices of the night.

A drive along the river offers 'close contact' impressions of wildlife and the African bush, while the tracks on top of the rocky ridges show a very different face of Tarangire: the tranquillity of the vast bush space of Africa. But there is one more 'jewel' which makes the picture even more complete: the 'Mbuga', the big swamp, in the south of the park.

Ulrich Döring

The African elephant, *Loxodonta africana*, will come across a mud puddle such as this, suck up water and then spray himself as his version of a bath. A couple of ways of telling elephants apart is by their tusks – shape, length, thickness, colouring or other marks – and their ears by checking the nicks and tears at the edges.

The Dwarf mongoose, *Helogale parvula*. Mongooses often inhabit old termite mounds such as this.

The African buffalo, *Syncerus caffer*, characterised by their huge bossed horns and general large size.

An elephant in a typical 'investigation' gesture. He is sucking air with our smell into his trunk and will then blow it into his mouth over the taste glands.

The African Mourning dove. *Streptopelia decipiens.*

The Maasai giraffe, *Giraffa camelopardalis.* When they get older they will occasionally become almost black all over.

Overleaf: Huge herds of elephants roam throughout the park at certain times of year. Elephants are incredibly sociable animals as well as being the largest land mammal in the world.

These lions are in the northern part of
the park. Tarangire has so much to offer the
visitor: the vast variety of wildlife, the beautiful
landscape and the often complete absence
of other visitors to the park.

Larmakau swamp at the southern
end of the park.

The sun sends firelight across the plains as it sets. This Baobab tree picks up the light and suddenly comes alive. With light comes life and rarely will a tree seem so vibrant.

Lake Manyara National Park

Although Lake Manyara is one of Tanzania's smallest National Parks, it is home to an extraordinary diversity of animal and plant life. Densely packed into an area of 330 sq km – approximately 230 km form the lake itself – the park is unique in its beauty and variety. Its name, Manyara, is derived from a Maasai word for a particular plant which is used in the making of very sturdy hedges!

The lake itself is obviously the park's primary attraction, and forms the most spectacular sight as one first enters the park gates. However, the several rivers around the lake are also of great interest, not least because they each have such individual characteristics and nourish such varying wildlife. Over the Msasa river delta, the bright colours of the pied kingfishers are always particularly eyecatching, as are their deft movements as they swoop down to the water, onto their unsuspecting prey. The Ndala river, south of the Msasa, often functions as a watering hole for elephants during the dry season, a time when the area around the Endabash river provides a home for many of the park's numerous animals. Also particularly worth a visit is the hippo pool, which forms part of the Simba river. Although the hippos should not be approached if they are found on land, watching them wallowing together in the water is quite a sight.

However, it is not only the lake and the many rivers which make the Manyara Park such an extraordinary place. Also very beautiful is the ground water forest. It shares many of the characteristics of the rain forest, which is the first habitat in which one finds oneself upon entering the park. The stunning variety and colour of its plant and animal life make a quite overwhelming first impression on the visitor.

Just south of the ground water forest is Mahali pa Nyati, the open spaciousness of which forms a striking contrast to the density of the forest. Although 'Mahali pa Nyati' actually means 'place of the buffalo', the visitor is rarely rewarded with any sightings of these particular animals, which tend to gather nearer the shores of the lake. However, the many herds of zebras and impala which roam the area more than compensate for this. In addition, if you are very lucky, you may catch an occasional glimpse of a lion lazing in the trees of the Acacia woodland. Lake Manyara is certainly a very special place.

A Common hippopotamus, *Hippopotamus amphibius*, yawns. This is often a threat display asserting dominance. Any disturbance in a pool of hippos will set off a barrage of yawning and honking.

At the hippo pool on the north end of Lake Manyara a small group of hippopotami fight. They don't often injure each other and, if they do sustain a cut or two, their hides are about 6cm thick so they will look worse than they actually feel.

As you drive along the west side of the lake
you cross many small streams. In the
dry season these become favourite haunts of
elephants because they provide so much
succulent fresh food.

Two male Olive baboons fight for dominance. There will be much charging, shaking, barking and baring of teeth to assert who is boss. But they rarely fight as it would be too dangerous with their incredibly sharp teeth.

Two female and a male ostrich, *Struthio camelus*, on the edge of the dried-up lake. The male, on the right, has black feathers and a pinker skin than the all over drab females.

Opposite: At the southern end of the park you will find Maji Moto Kubwa or Big Hot Water (a pedantic literal translation sounding like the name of an Indian Chief; the non-literal translation would be Big Hot Springs). The water emerges from the ground at about 60°C and flows off into the lake.

A female impala drinks from a very depleted stream. In the wet season this stream will fill up.

Elephants will occasionally reach up with their trunks to get at the very young and fresh shoots emerging on branches high up. They are also known to stand up on their hind legs to reach up, but will only do this if they are unable to knock the tree down themselves – which they are inclined to do if the tree is small enough.

A row of Common wildebeest or White-bearded gnus, *Connochaetes taurinus*, stand on the hot and dry Lake Manyara.

Ngorongoro Conservation Area

Writing of Ngorongoro, the late Professor Bernhard Grzimek stated, 'It is impossible to give a fair description of the size and beauty of the crater, for there is nothing with which one can compare it. It is one of the Wonders of the World.'

The Ngorongoro Conservation Area, a World Heritage Site, at the centre of which the crater lies, is indeed an extraordinary place, and perhaps the most spectacular natural reserve for the visitor to Tanzania. Not only is it home to a vast array of wildlife, but it also boasts an enormous wealth of archaeological sites, showing evidence of human habitation spanning millions of years. In fact, living in the Eyasi basin, to the south of the Conservation Area, are the Hadza people, whose culture and language may represent vestiges of a lifestyle prototypical of early mankind.

However, for those not fascinated by archaeological history, there is more than enough plant and wildlife to keep any visitor busy, from the Northern Highlands to the Serengeti Plain. A drive through the forest reserve, in the south-east of the Conservation Area, as well as being uplifting in itself, offers extraordinary views of the crater, at about 2200 m above sea level. What is most amazing about the crater itself is the great variety of habitats which it encompasses, allowing it to support a wealth of different wildlife.

It would be a pity to visit Ngorongoro without taking a drive in the crater itself to see this abundant animal life. Not only are there eagles and buzzards flying above the crater, but on the ground you will see zebras, gazelles, gnus, rhinoceros, lions and the rather less glamourous warthog! A visit to the Lerai forest also offers glimpses of wildlife as varied as elephants, waterbuck, eland and baboons.

The Olmoti Crater, north of Ngorongoro, is home to the beautiful Munge Stream, which, as it leaves the crater, cascades hundreds of metres down the cliffs, forming a stunning waterfall. Just north of Olmoti Crater is the Empakaai Crater, a mysterious and densely forested area which, with a deep lake in the bottom, is a favourite haunt of flamingos. In stark contrast to the abundance in these craters are the dry Serengeti and Sale Plains, which form about half of the total Conservation Area. Although somewhat bleak and daunting to the visitor, these plains have a pure, clean beauty of their own. They also boast the extraordinary Nasera Rock, which rises about 100 m above the ground, affording a wonderful view of the surrounding landscape and the Shifting Sands, a dune of lava sand which moves small distances each year towards the west.

It is, however, impossible to do justice to the magnificent landscape of the Ngorongoro Conservation Area in an introduction as brief as this; it is, indeed, an area which has to be seen to be believed.

Ngorongoro Crater

The Ngorongoro Conservation Area (NCA) has many different features, but probably the best known is the Ngorongoro Crater, a huge volcanic caldera teeming with wildlife attracting people from all over the world all year round. This means there are many places to stay around the rim of the crater, although one of the options is to camp, getting close to nature and the animals.

We camped in Simba campsite, shown here, and pitched our tents on the edge of the site near the bushes. That night went fine apart from the extreme cold! In the morning, however, I noticed my two travelling companions acting slightly nervously. Apparently we'd had a visit from an elephant during the night. This was fine by me, in fact it was quite exciting – easy to say from the position of a Landrover roof tent! My two friends, in their two-man ground-level tent, were less amused. Anyway, many jokes later, we left on safari into the crater, leaving Ally in the camp and forgetting about the morning's excitement. Until, that is, we arrived back at the campsite to find Ally, our brave and fearless friend, had moved our camp right into the middle of the site, amidst many other happy campers. Ally looked very sheepish and went into lengthy safety explanations. Herman and I could hardly stand up for laughing, and poor Ally had to endure lots of 'coward' jokes all evening.

A view of the crater as you descend the 600 m to the bottom. In the middle distance on the crater floor is Lake Makat or Lake Magadi. *Makat* is Maasai for soda, *magadi* is Swahili for soda.

81

The NCA, as opposed to the National Parks, has human residents. These are the Maasai people who are predominantly pastoralists and will bring their cattle, donkeys, sheep and goats into the crater to water them. You might imagine that their cattle would be easy prey for any of the crater's many resident predators, but most of the predators, especially lions, are well aware of the kudos if a Maasai kills one of them.

As well as using water to bathe, elephants will use dust. They suck it up with their trunk and blow it over themselves; this also keeps the flies away.

Lake Makat is host to a wide variety of creatures, mainly water birds but also hippos. The level of the water will rise and fall, sometimes quite dramatically, according to the season.

Ngorongoro Crater

The lion population of the Ngorongoro Crater has undergone some quite dramatic changes. In 1962 the population of lions in the crater was decimated by biting flies to about 15. Over the following years the numbers built up again to 70-100. Until 1995 that is, when a viral disease cut the population back down to around 35. Since then the numbers of lions in the crater have increased but it will take years again to reach the same numbers.

Lesser flamingos, which only come to Lake Makat to feed, will return to Lake Natron to rest and breed.

In the dry season sand storms get whipped up around Lake Makat and sometimes, late into the day, clouds will remain on the crater rim.

The crater is also full of plains game, such as these wildebeest running in the familiar linear formation. The wildebeest of the crater are resident here, so they don't migrate like their neighbours in the Serengeti.

A few zebra walk on the edge of Lake Makat amidst the tyre tracks of the many other vehicles in the crater. There are, and always will be, many other vehicles in the crater. It is an awesome place, so there are bound to be, but it needn't spoil your trip – it certainly didn't for us.

Left: Elephants are a fairly common sight in the crater, although you will rarely see large family groups as most of these elephants are wandering bachelors.

At Mandusi swamp you will find the ubiquitous hippo pool. A fine spot to watch a variety of birds and carefully study the energetic movements of the hippos.

The crater rim and Engitati Hill and a couple of elephants.

North of Ngorongoro Crater, there are two more craters: Olmoti and Empakaai. This is a view of Empakaai Crater as you descend to the bottom. The lake in the crater is about 85 m deep – exceptionally deep for a crater lake. It hosts flamingos, Egyptian geese and many other water birds. We also saw evidence of hyena and bushbuck. The lake at the bottom has quite an eerie feel about it, possibly due to misty weather and the place being devoid of any other visitors, very strange compared with Ngorongoro Crater.

Olduvai Gorge, in the western part of the NCA, runs for about 50 km, is named after the Maasai word for wild sisal, '*Oldupai*'. It is in this gorge that Professor Kanttwinkel discovered the first fossils in 1911. Following his return to Berlin, Professor Reck was in 1913 inspired by Kanttwinkel's work to go and look for himself. The work was halted by the war but was restarted by Reck and Louis Leakey in 1931. Reck later handed over the rights for excavation to Leakey who, with his wife Mary, proceeded to Olduvai when funds allowed. It was in 1959 that Mary Leakey discovered a fossilized skull belonging to *Australopithecus boisei* – about 1.75 million years old. Following this highly significant discovery, they were enabled to continue the work and proceeded to make many more vital discoveries, such as fossil footprints over 3 million years old, found at a place called Laetoli – by far the oldest hominid footprints ever found. (See Introduction.)

In the gorge at the place Mary Leakey discovered *Australopithecus boisei*. This plaque, with an assortment of fossilised bones around it, reminds us of the immense hard work and perseverance of the Leakeys and the significance of their discoveries.

MARA

*M*ara region derives its name from the Mara river which flows from Kenya and pours into Lake Victoria near Musoma Town. The Mara river is well known amongst wildlife enthusiasts as one of the rivers where you can see thousands of wildebeest crossing while they move in the Great Migration, a magnificent sight which also occurs in the Grumeti river in Mara region in the Serengeti's Western Corridor.

Mara is one of the smallest regions on mainland Tanzania and made smaller by having Lake Victoria cutting off its west side and with the Serengeti National Park taking up a large bulk of the east side. Without knowing it, most people who visit the Serengeti are paying a visit to Mara region when they reach Seronera in the heart of the Serengeti. So although very few visitors actually reach Musoma, the capital of Mara, thousands upon thousands of people each year come to Mara region.

Musoma, as the administrative centre for Mara region, is a small town on the shores of Lake Victoria. It has an easy air of somewhere not overcome with the stresses of day-to-day life. It is very easy to relax at one of the new small hotels there and watch the sun set over the lake. The major activity of Mara region is fishing, both on the large and small scale. Although the fish factories are not as prolific or as large as those found in Mwanza, they are still working and filleting Nile perch, freezing them and exporting them. The other small-scale-fishing is usually for tilapia and is mostly eaten by the fishermen and their families.

In the region you will also encounter a certain amount of agriculture; ranging from maize, beans and finger millet which are all used for eating. The millet is used to make a version of ugali, a thick edible substance which, when made from millet, is an appetising brown colour and when made with ground maize flour is a white colour. The other main crop in Mara is cotton. Grown as a cash crop, it is used to pay for school fees or any other expenses.

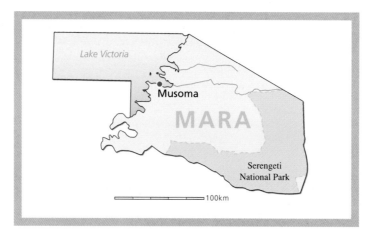

Mara has several ethnic groups, some of which are small and inter-related. The Luo people are found in both Mara and across the border in Nyanza province in Kenya. The Kurya, Shashi, Ikizu and Zanaki are also from the Mara region. Former President 'Mwalimu' Julius Nyerere is from the Zanaki people and used to tell many Zanaki stories and legends to illustrate his speeches. Mara, though small, has much to offer the visitor from the vast plains of the Serengeti to the beautiful shores of Lake Victoria. If given the opportunity, take it, and visit Musoma and its surrounding landscape.

Musoma main street.

After cotton has been ginned and made ready for export, Musoma is one of the ports from which it will travel. The bales of cotton are loaded onto the barges by fork-lift truck – if it works.

The *Thor* is being loaded with cotton. When full, it will sail to Mwanza where the cotton will be loaded onto a train destined for Dar es Salaam, from where it will be exported.

Lake Victoria has two main varieties of fish: tilapia and Nile perch. These gentlemen are probably fishing for tilapia, as it is both more tasty and easier to catch with a small rod. Nile perch can reach 70-80 kilos!

Charlie, in the blue T-shirt and cap, and his mate Peter, in the shorts, were taking out the rubbish and were only too delighted to stop for a chat and a couple of pictures.

Serengeti National Park

Serengeti is perhaps the most famous of East Africa's National Parks – and deservedly so. The largest park in Tanzania, it stretches along a high plateau from the border with Kenya towards Lake Victoria, and was first established as a National Park in 1951. Serengeti is renowned for its many and spectacular plains in the south-east, which are home to a vast community of animals. However, the northern, more mountainous area is equally spectacular, as is the Acacia savannah in the heart of the park.

Indeed, the first view of the plains upon entering Serengeti justifies their fame. They are at their most striking if visited in the months of May and June, at the outset of the dry season, the time of the great annual wildebeest migration. At this time, vast numbers of wildebeest gather together for the trek to the woodland, to watch them as they all speed north is breathtakingly impressive. As well as the wildebeest, the Serengeti plains are home to a vast array of animal life: the hyena, the cheetah, the zebra, the gazelle, the leopard and the elephant, to name but a few.

Seronera Valley, in the heart of Serengeti, is renowned for its fine population of lions and leopards, who tend not to favour the open grassland of the plains. While lions always live in communities, the leopard is essentially a solitary animal, yet the relative abundance of both in this area ensures sightings of each. The vervet, a small breed of monkey, and the baboon, which tends to live in sometimes ramblingly large troops, are also in evidence.

Moving further north, one reaches Banagi, home to the giraffe and to herds of impala and buffalo. Not far from Banagi, at Retima, is a hippo pool – always worth a visit to see the cumbersomely weighty hippos as they dive into the water, rising to the surface for noisy inhalations of air.

Passing on from Banagi, one covers some of the world's oldest rock formations, mined for gold until the mid 1960s. However, now that Serengeti is protected from such activities, this area can be appreciated simply for its stunning natural beauty, its spectacular open grassland, hills and woodland.

The main road from Arusha to Mwanza runs straight through the Serengeti which means you can, in effect, get a cheap game drive from the bus. The journey does take about 20 hours though.

In the heart of the Serengeti is Seronera. This area encompasses the HQ of the park and all its various facilities, garage, staff accommodation, visitors centre, airstrip, etc – and there is a lodge and a collection of campsites. Seronera is named after the river that flows through the area and you can see the Seronera, Ngare Nanyuki and Nyabogati rivers, defined by the trees running along their courses.

Seronera is well known as a fine game viewing spot, especially for leopards. Never having seen a leopard in the wild before I was enthusiastically craning my neck at every yellow barked acacia tree, because we all know that's really where they live… Anyone who has ever been leopard spotting will know exactly what I mean. Finally near the end of a rather fruitless leopard search this is what I see: Leopard, *Panthera pardus*.

A lion cub sneaks forward to investigate the visitors to his area. Finally unsure what to make of us, he turns round and chases his tail just to reassure himself.

Cheetahs, *Acinonyx jubatus*, are the fastest mammals on the planet, able to run up to speeds of 90-112 kph (60-70 mph), although they lack the stamina of the wild dogs. Due to their speed and use of it for catching prey, they need wide open spaces such as this area near Simba Kopjes.

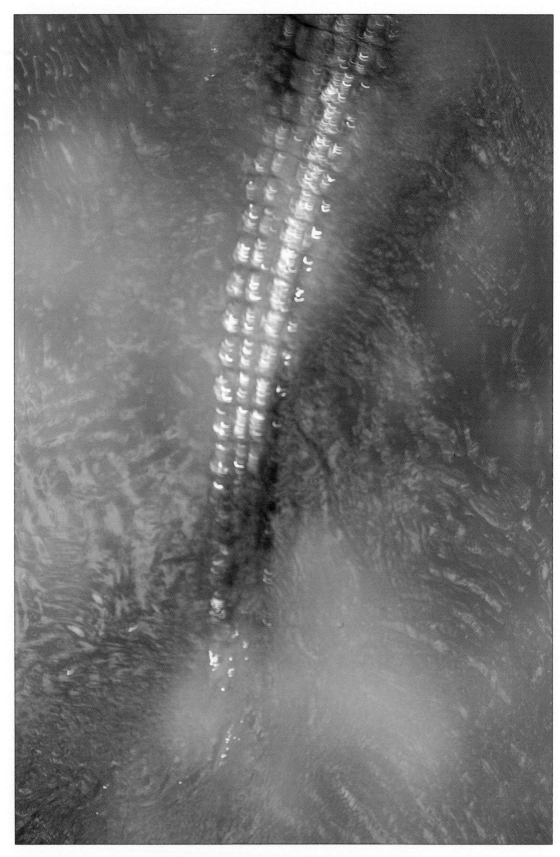

Standing on a small rickety bridge over the Grumeti
River in the Western Corridor of the Serengeti, I felt, as
I lent over to snap the croc as it passed underneath me,
that at least I'd get something different if it was to be
my last photograph. I survived to fight another day.

The Grumeti River and its small tributaries play host to many crocodiles, *Crocodilus niloticus*. In migration time, when the Corridor is absolutely flooded with wildebeest trying to cross rivers, the crocodiles have a feast. Apart from drowned animals to feed on they will also attack and take off wildebeest still swimming the river.

We saw these lions up this sausage tree, *Kigalia aethiopica*, in Seronera. They are probably in the tree for its shade. Despite many assertions to the contrary all lions will climb trees if so inclined.

The Serengeti is home to the massive migrations of wildebeest and zebra. The migration is in the Western Corridor around May, June and July and starts to move north after that towards the Mara in Kenya. This Common wildebeest or White-bearded gnu, is jumping a stream on his way to join the rest, all heading north.

Overleaf: The early morning sees us back in the Western Corridor watching the noisy and quite fantastic herds of wildebeest move northwards.

On the edge of the park near Naabi Hill, there is a small rocky kopje which was at this time bed for this tired gentleman. A male lion, *Panthera leo*; he had quite likely been mating recently. Firstly, he looks absolutely exhausted and secondly, there was a smiling lioness asleep not very far away.

In the southern part of the park around Lake Ndutu, bordering on the Ngorongoro Conservation Area, we saw these three elephants, probably a mother with her two children. Due to the matriarchal nature of the elephant social system, it is only the young males who will leave the original family; related females will stay together for generations.

A cheetah having just eaten, rests on top of a granite kopje in the Simba Kopjes.

As a way of viewing game and experiencing the African bush, there can be few ways, if any, more peaceful and ecologically friendly than floating above the earth in a hot air balloon. The champagne breakfast one indulges in after the flight is wonderful but it does make you feel like doing what that cheetah over there is doing, for the whole day.

MWANZA

After Dar es Salaam, Mwanza is probably the next busiest commercial centre in Tanzania. It has a unique atmosphere, with Lake Victoria contributing a lot, making it a busy, bustling town and yet relaxed, like many of the coastal towns.

Mwanza town is the capital of Mwanza region, half of which is in Lake Victoria and includes the Ukerewe and Ukara islands and the idyllic Rubondo Island National Park, the other half in the fertile and well watered lands around the southern part of the lake.

The region is mainly populated by the Sukuma people who also live in Shinyanga and the northern parts of the Tabora region. The Sukuma are the most populous group in Tanzania.

Lake Victoria features prominently in the lives of the people of Mwanza region. Boats that ply the lake make it possible for Mwanza to be in touch with Bukoba in the west of the lake and with Kisumu in Kenya and Port Bell in Uganda. Boat transport on Lake Victoria is quite efficient and regular – the tragic MV *Bukoba* accident in May 1996, in which about 1,000 people perished when the boat sunk just outside Mwanza, is the first of its kind and has been followed by a greatly increased awareness of safety precautions on the part of boat operators and passengers alike.

Much fishing goes on in Mwanza region and the fillets of the Nile perch are exported from Mwanza to various countries in Europe. Most of the fishing is done by gill-nets and, apart from the Nile perch, tilapia is also quite popular in Mwanza. The recent infestation of Lake Victoria waters with the water hyacinth has caused concern to local fishermen, governmental and non-government environmental bodies, as well as scientists, on how to eradicate the weed without harming other lake life.

Rubondo Island National Park is relatively small and yet incredibly diverse in what it offers the visitor. Like a few other parks in Tanzania, its isolation means few visitors – a combination offering a quite superb experience. Game drive by boat or foot and you will see a huge variety of animals and birds. The authorities are also in the process of habituating chimpanzees which were introduced to the park.

The region has other islands in Lake Victoria: Kome, Maisome, Saanane, Ukerewe and Ukara islands, which all have great potential for development for tourism.

Mwanza region is well known for growing cotton and thus has ginneries scattered around the region.

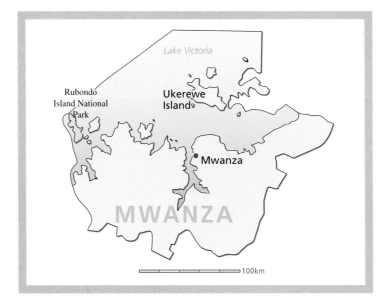

The area around Mwanza Town is littered with granite boulders and Bismarck Rock, seen here beyond the canoe, is certainly the most impressive.

The bustling main street in Mwanza.

MV Victoria unloading some vital supplies. The *MV Victoria* calls at Bukoba, Kisumu in Kenya and Port Bell in Uganda. It carries both passengers and freight.

Faustin makes sloping-topped fence posts. His company also makes bricks; he says it is better not to have all your bricks in one pallet!

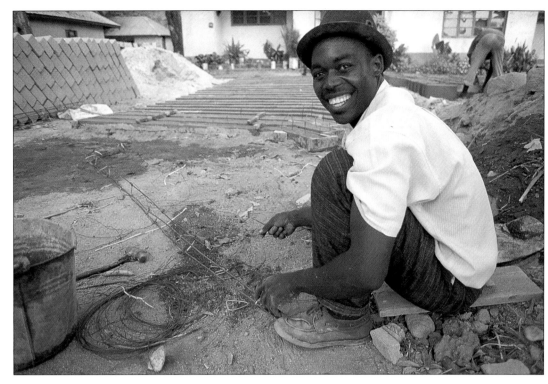

The train is one of the better ways of travelling to this part of the country, especially in the rainy season when many of the roads become impassable. Trains go to Tabora from here and then either go west to Kigoma or east to Dodoma and Dar es Salaam.

A brave soul decides to shift his pickup from Ukerewe Island to Mwanza. Nansio is the main town on Ukerewe Island, which is only a couple of hours ferry trip from Mwanza. The ferry is a passenger boat as opposed to a car ferry, which makes it that much more exciting to move vehicles backwards and forwards!

Mama Barome smiles beautifully, possibly due to good sales in Nansio this afternoon due to the imminent arrival of the Mwanza ferry.

Throughout Tanzania various foods are sold on the side of the road to quench that insidious thirst or hunger and here are a couple of fine examples: oranges and dried 'dagaa', little fish like whitebait. After eating these you are defied to be either hungry or thirsty.

Beat a drum not a child
the rights of children first
Children's rights are top of the agenda
on a street in Nansio, Ukerewe.

An unsuspecting farmer lays out his cassava to dry on an unused cement
floor only to find an errant goat is eating it! Fortunately on this occasion the
undeserving goat was chased off fairly sharpish by a young lad.

At the Farai ginnery in Mwanza the raw cotton is brought from all over the region by Primary Co-operative Societies. It is loaded into a ware-house then sucked through a large pipe into the gin itself. Here you see a worker pushing some raw cotton into the pipe and holding off the rest with his back to stop it clogging up.

The raw cotton is then dropped here above the separators and is moved along to be pushed down into the actual gins.

The separators divide the pure cotton from its seed.

The tramper compresses the clean cotton into bales and subsequently wraps and binds it ready for export.

Cotton seed has various uses: often it is donated back to the farmers to aid subsequent crops; alternatively it is crushed and used to make oil. Here the seed is being loaded into an oil factory.

Rubondo Island National Park

Rubondo Island National Park is actually made up of one main island, Rubondo Island, and its satellite islands in Lake Victoria. The park offers a completely different safari experience. You start in a boat – which is a fairly unusual vehicle for animal viewing – and you are offered an amazing spectacle of crocodiles, hippopotamus, lizards, the elusive sitatunga, giraffe and a plethora of birds. The range of animals in this park, which protects 240 sq kms, is quite spectacular. When you leave the boat and go on foot, you may be lucky and see various species of monkey – including chimpanzees. These were introduced, alongside giraffe, black and white colobus, black rhino, suni, roan antelope, porcupine and elephant, in the 60s and 70s to diversify the park's already wide range of wildlife. Although the rhino hasn't been seen for years, the other animals introduced have settled well in Rubondo. Some of them are harder to see than others but the park is currently working with the Frankfurt Zoological Society to habituate the chimpanzees. It will take about another two years before they are easy to view.

One blight which affects most National Parks is poaching, here taking the form of illegal fishing. The National Park stretches out into the lake about a kilometre and it is illegal to fish within this boundary. However because of the ban, the fish naturally proliferate – and this occasionally proves too tempting! The ranger posts throughout the park are littered with what used to be poachers' boats.

The park is developing rapidly and tourist facilities are improving with a good tented camp and cheaper options run by the park. The hope is that more and more people will enjoy such a completely different wildlife experience.

Opposite: A tree completely denuded of its living bits by birds of all descriptions. The luckier tree behind is harbouring a flock of Sacred ibis, *Threskiornis aethiopicus.*

Maasai giraffe were brought here in 1965 as one of the first animals to be introduced
into the park. They are seen here on the main island, Rubondo.

Around the main island of the park are many small islands where you can see hundreds
of animals, reptiles and birds. The crocodile is commonly seen, although they are quite shy,
and will run into the water as you approach.

The African fish eagle, *Haliaeetus vocifer*, commonly seen around rivers and lakes throughout East Africa, is a very successful fish hunter. After flying around above the water, it will spot a fish near the surface and then dive and grab the fish with its claws. Its feet have rough pads to facilitate grabbing the slippery fish. The eagle is seen here after just having caught a fish. Occasionally they grab a fish which is too large and either drop it or, if they can't release the fish, they get pulled down and drown.

The rangers taking me around had earlier found a poachers' boat hidden in the reeds around 'Miti Mirefu' or 'Tall Trees' area so they were aware that there was probably a fishing line lurking somewhere. They were not disappointed. Respichios pulled it in.

This was what the poacher was hoping for: a pair of fairly good sized Nile perch, *Lates niloticus*. Live fish are used as bait and the method is quite effective. The line is extremely long and takes almost an hour to pull in.

In the forest on Rubondo Island we sadly didn't see any elephants but there was evidence of their delicate activities everywhere.

The highly elusive sitatunga, *Tragelphus spekii*, is mainly a swamp dweller and not often seen. They are genetically close to the bushbuck and could be mistaken for one, except that the horns on the sitatunga are longer and more curved. In this park they frequent the water's edge but will venture inland to eat other vegetation during the night or late in the day, as seen here.

The little egret, *Egretta garzetta*, often found around the shores of the islands.

'Kisiwa cha Ndege' or Bird Island, aptly named due to its bird population which has done a fine job of relieving the trees of most of their leaves and carpeting the island in white – giving it a very eerie feel. The island is about 100 meters in diameter and its residents include crocodiles, monitor lizards and birds.

Opposite: The sun sets behind the palm trees of Rubondo Island.

KAGERA

With lots of sunshine and frequent and heavy thunderstorms, Kagera region is a lushly verdant land with patches of primeval equatorial forests, particularly in the mountainous areas bordering the Kagera National Park in Rwanda. Lake Victoria is the major physical feature of the Kagera region and until after the war that drove out the invading armies of Uganda's Idi Amin from the Kagera area in 1979, the region had been known as West Lake region.

Before and after the war the relationship between the people of Kagera region and their fellows across the border in Uganda have been very cordial. Trade across the border continues to be very brisk and the languages on either side of the border are similar. Kagera region gets its electricity from the Owen Falls in Uganda. Bukoba shopkeepers find it easier to get their provisions from Kampala and rumour has it that not all of Bukoba's robusta coffee finds its way to Dar es Salaam. East African co-operation does make better sense to the people of Kagera region than to the bureaucrats and politicians in Dar es Salaam or Dodoma.

Kagera's robusta coffee is grown among banana plants in small family groves. These groves are constantly fertilized by manure and carefully tended. Beans are also intercropped with the bananas and coffee, adding to the fertility of the soil. There is presently no important cash crop other than robusta coffee. The Kagera sugar factory was destroyed by the Amin invaders in 1978, and it never managed to come back to full production after that. The instant coffee factory in Bukoba still produces coffee which is distributed throughout East Africa.

Kagera region has been plagued by several misfortunes: The Amin invasion and the war that followed saw combat on Tanzanian soil and the region is one the worst places in Tanzania to be hit by the AIDS pandemic. Happily, Kagera region was also the first to accept the reality of AIDS and take serious and active measures to educate the people about it. The results of this positive effort are already showing. In May 1996 the MV *Bukoba*, which had taken off from Bukoba via Kemondo Bay sailing overnight to Mwanza, capsized within sight of the town drowning nearly 1,000 passengers, most of whom were from Kagera region.

Despite tragedies such as this, Kagera people remain deeply committed to the development of their region – maintaining their culture and language with dedication exceptional even compard with other groups in Tanzania.

The Haya people are more frequently associated with Kagera region but many other groups claim Kagera as their home region. Some such groups are: the Nyambo, Subi, Ha, Hangaza, Sumbwa, Zinza, and a relatively new group that is a mixture of the Baganda and Haya called the Gandakyaka.

Kagera is the main region for robusta coffee and this is a cooperative society buying station. The coffee is brought here, weighed and the farmers are paid.

After coffee is harvested it is dried and subsequently cleaned in the farm. This is a store where they are loading the dried coffee cherries into bags so they can load the cleaning machine.

Kemondo Bay is the other port, apart from Bukoba, that services Kagera region. Kagera's coffee is shipped from here by boat to Mwanza and then by train to Tanga or Dar es Salaam where it is exported.

In Kemondo Bay there is a warehouse used to store coffee by the company Mazao Limited, based in Moshi. The head of their security for the Kagera region is Mzee Jumbe.

Bukoba, on the shores of Lake Victoria and very near the border with Uganda, has good access to both Kenya and Uganda as well as to Mwanza on the southern shores of Lake Victoria.

The tower of the Jamatini Mosque in Bukoba.

Overleaf: Housing differs from town to town, but Bukoba is the first town in which I have seen housing like this.

125

On Kashozi Road in Bukoba, Fortunata Rweyemanu does her best to make a living selling things from her small *duka* or shop. She told me she got the *duka* in 1990 and has survived on it since then, although sometimes the going can be tough.

On the street side in Bukoba a few seamstresses work away under the protective shade of kangas. The ladies, left to right, Savelina, Deodata and Rosemary complained that the only major problem of working on the street, as it were, was the midday sun.

On the shores of Lake Victoria you are very likely to meet these fellows in their droves – lake flies. They look not dissimilar to mosquitoes and have been known to cause panic in the unsuspecting visitor who sees a massive swarm of apparent mossies. Actually they are harmless and quite tasty to eat, fried.

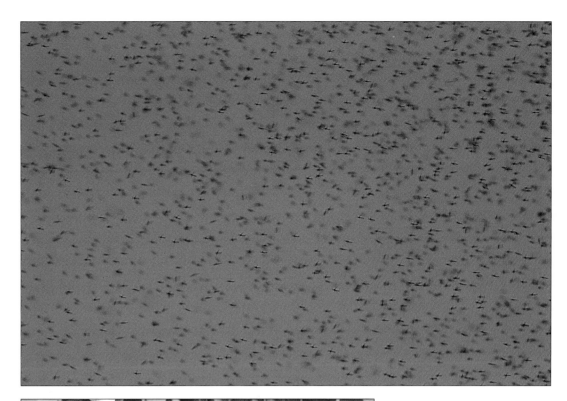

Plantain bananas are a staple diet in this area. People steam and eat them as 'matoke' in a style similar to Ugandans, their close neighbours.

Benaco Refugee Camp, Ngara.

In June 1994 the Ngara district, in Kagera region in northern Tanzania, broke out onto world TV screens as hundreds of thousands of Rwandans flooded over the border at the Rusomo bridge crossing. A site marked out as a transit centre on Benaco hill soon came to be talked about as the largest refugee camp in the world. Images of blue and white plastic sheeting came to symbolise the plight of the thousands who had fled Rwanda as a consequence of the spread of the civil war and the genocide. A whole population of people found themselves suddenly having to cope in their flimsy huts huddled together on the edge of a bleak hill. Much of the burden was shouldered by the local Tanzanians as the social and environmental costs increasingly became apparent. The Rwandan camps lasted for two and a half years before the refugees were repatriated, but Tanzania continues to play host to refugee influxes. During the mid and late 1990s both the Kagera and Kigoma regions have become home to new refugees (from Burundi and the Democratic Republic of Congo) and, with continuing instability in the region, the likelihood of large population displacements remains.

SIMON LARKIN, RELIEF WORKER

Simon, who worked for two relief agencies in Ngara and in a camp for Congolese in Kigoma region, later reflected "working in these camps leaves heavy impressions. It is a world of extremes; the vastness of the population suddenly living in such precarious circumstances, the trauma, fear and suspicion of ordinary people fleeing the conflict, the pain of separation or loss of your family contrasts with moments of inspiration – groups sharing and supporting each other, teachers and parents organising their children's education, literacy classes attended by hundreds and so on. Men and women creatively building a life out of nothing as the human spirit flourishes over despair and despondency".

SHINYANGA

Gold and diamonds, cotton and cattle – all this wealth comes from Shinyanga region, making it one of the best endowed regions of Tanzania.

Shinyanga is accessible by road from Musoma, Bukoba and Mwanza in the north and from Dodoma, Singida and Tabora in the south. A railway-line passes Shinyanga on its way to Mwanza. Shinyanga town is itself unremarkable, apart from being one of the centres of the cotton industry, collecting the cash crop from small-holders and ginneries for hundreds of miles around and transporting it to Dar es Salaam for export. A small part of the cotton is used in the cloth factories which have now begun to run again after the massive privatisation that began in the mid 1990s. One can also travel to Shinyanga by air landing at the small airport at Mwadui, about 20 km north-east of Shinyanga.

The Sukuma are the major group of people living in Shinyanga. They are a hard-working lot but also very ebullient and full of song and dance. Not only are the Sukuma great cultivators of cotton but also keepers of livestock which thrive well in Shinyanga due to the absence of tsetse flies. Sukuma herds rival those of the Maasai, which accounts for the frequent clashes between the Maasai and the Sukuma over cattle rustling. The Maasai believe it is God Himself who decreed them to be the exclusive keepers of cattle. Sukuma men consider cattle to be the only meaningful sign of wealth, and the legal tender for payment of dowries – a man may pay as many as 40 head of cattle for a beautiful bride. Some of the clashes between the Maasai and Sukuma herdsmen have had to be stopped by officers of the Stock Theft Police Unit, a special police branch set up to deal with cattle rustling.

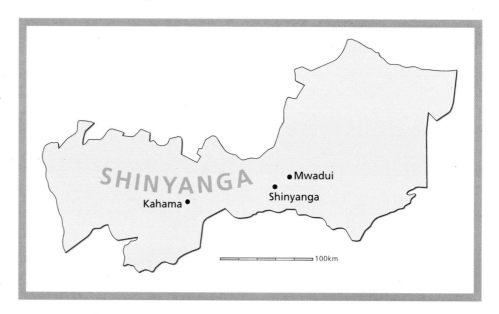

Diamonds abound in Shinyanga and stories have it that the hard, shiny stones were popular pieces for the *bao* game played by elderly Sukuma men until the late 1930s when diamonds were first mined commercially in the region.

Serengeti National Park stretches into the region for more than 50 km and, from where it ends, the Maswa Game Reserve sticks out westwards for another 50 km. These wildlands are less frequently visited than the eastern and northern parts of the Serengeti, and so they are preserved as they were in times gone by.

A young lad drives his cattle happily along the railway track. The trains coming along this track would, of course, stop when they saw the cattle.

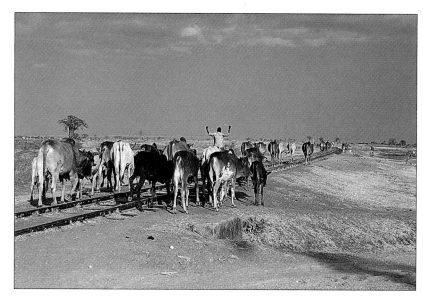

On March 6, 1940, Dr. John Williamson, a Canadian mining geologist discovered the Mwadui diamond deposits. By 19 March 1942, he had established a private company, Williamson Diamonds Limited. On his death in 1958 the then Tanganyika Government and De Beers Consolidated Mines took over as joint owners. The mine was privatised in 1994 with De Beers owning 75% of the shares and a 16 million dollar rehabilitation programme was undertaken.

It is the largest open-cast diamond mine in the world. The 'pipe' is the lava tube that rises from the depths of the earth and spreads out at the earth's crust, thus revealing diamonds. The 'pipe' at Mwadui is 1.5 km on its long axis and 1 km on its short axis. The area it covers is 146 hectares. The pit hasn't been mined for some years because they have been mining the 'superficial' ore. This picture shows the one side of the pit with the new treatment plant in the distance.

All around the pit is what's called 'superficial' ore, i.e. not mining the pipe but all that is around it. Here is a dumper truck receiving ore from a dragline.

The ore is shifted into these scrubber bins before moving into the actual scrubbers, where the ore is scrubbed in water and then screened to separate the product into particles greater than 1.5mm and less than 25mm.

From the scrubbers the ore passes through various stages of crushing, cleaning and separation until it reaches this area. This is the dense media seperator which sorts the concentrate which holds the diamonds into a special container which is subsequently transported to the recovery room for further sorting. Also it sends the 'tailings' (ordinary rocks and stones) by conveyor, seen at the front of the picture, off up to the tailings dump.

Diamond mining is not always on a grand scale (This is a diamond mine.) It belongs to the gentleman shown here, Charles Beno Ngonyani. He is one of many residents of Maganzo near Mwadui, who mines his own diamonds in his back yard. They get small amounts for the diamonds they find as they are mostly of industrial as opposed to gem quality.

Bwana Sita harvesting his cotton. He will sell his cotton to the local co-operative society to get cash to make any new purchases, send children to school or pay for medical expenses, all of which are painfully expensive. He also farms maize and millet for his own consumption.

TABORA

Tabora region was originally known as the 'Unyamwezi', its people being called the Nyamwezi. Tabora town, originally known as Unyanyembe, has seen greater days. In the 1800s, Tabora was the most important interior town on the Bagamoyo-Ujiji caravan route. Salt from Uvinza in the north-west was brought to Tabora for trade, and so was copper from Katanga. Tabora was also the collection point for ivory, a commodity that had unique importance in long-distance trade.

The first caravan from Tabora reached the coast in about 1800. By 1830, it was usual to see caravans, with as many as one thousand people from Tabora, snaking their way along the route that has now been taken by the central railway-line going to the coast, laden with ivory, beeswax, copper, foodstuffs and other trading commodities.

Tabora was well connected to the trade conducted by the Yao in the south of Tanzania, and with the famous Tippu Tib, whose proper name was Hamed ibn Mohammed, the Afro-Arab whose father married the daughter of Chief Fundikira of Unyanyembe. Some Nyamwezi traders grew to great fame and fortune in the long-distance trade and one such was Msiri whose proper name was Ngelengwa. Msiri went to Katanga in the 1850 and carved out a huge personal empire founded on the long distance trade.

The great Mirambo and Nyungu ya Mawe together controlled all what is now Tabora region as well as parts of Rukwa and Singida regions, controlling the long distance trade to the coast. The two leaders died in 1884 and their empires were greatly reduced after their death.

Present-day Tabora is a lot quieter than the Tabora of Mirambo and Nyungu ya Mawe. The town is dotted with huge ancient mango trees which were grown by the long distance traders, making the streets shady and cool. One of the main features of today's Tabora is the station. With the town being fairly isolated, with few roads, rail-travel for people and goods is the most convenient way to get about. Thus any time a train comes into town the station it hums with action.

The Nyamwezi are people who cultivate cotton and tobacco as cash crops as well as keeping livestock. They have retained the friendly, cosmopolitan ways of their widely travelled forefathers.

Tabora is also well known for its honey and beeswax produced by the Tabora Beekeepers Co-operative Society. It is worth noting that the honey and beeswax is still exported along the same routes as it was in the 1800s although these days it goes mostly by train and so is likely to arrive at its destination a great deal quicker.

The sun sets over a busy street in Tabora town.

Tabora is in the very heart of Tanzania in a tricky area for travelling by road. Although perfectly feasible in the dry season it will take you days to get anywhere. Thus the train is the best option. The train goes through Tabora on the way to Kigoma, or up to Mwanza or along to Dodoma and Dar es Salaam. For example, if you wanted to get to Kigoma by car it would take you a minimum of two and a half days solid driving. Much quicker by train!

Small scale concerns makes up a large portion of all industry. Here they are making watering cans for sale locally.

This is what the road looks like when you drive out of Tabora south through Tutubu and Ipole. It is a sand road which is not bad in the dry season and it goes on interminably until you forget that Tanzania has any other kind of landscape. If you are lucky, you eventually arrive at Mpanda in Rukwa region

KIGOMA

*K*igoma used to be one of the more economically depressed regions in Tanzania. This stems from the early colonial days when it was decided that Kigoma as a region should not have a cash crop economy so that its people could be recruited as labour for the settler plantations in the east and the north of the country. Kigoma's most numerous people, the Ha, were seen to be hard working and loyal.

Oil palms grow very well in virtually the whole of the region, but palm oil extraction has not gone far beyond domestic and small-scale industrial production.

Ujiji, Kigoma's elder sister town and only a few kilometres away, has a lot of historical and architectural interest. The history of Ujiji goes back more than two hundred years. It is a small town that reveals a strong Islamic and Arabic influence – and is renowned in the Islamic world by the devotion and erudition of its sheikhs. It was here that Stanley and Livingstone met, and Ujiji predates Kigoma town which, like Moshi, grew around a railway station.

The little town of Uvinza, with a history even older than Ujiji, lies south-east of Kigoma, on the railway-line, and is traversed by the road running south from Uganda to Zambia and Zaire. Both road and railway trace routes of ancient pathways from the coast, from the Kingdom of Bugunda and beyond – the central African kingdoms and from little remembered villages and communities – to Uvinza, 'the place of salt', to obtain this valuable commoditiy. Uvinza salt comes from the Uvinza spring and archaeological excavation has shown that the spring was being worked one thousand years ago. Today, Uvinza is still productive, and remains one of Tanzania's biggest sources of salt, using the same routes as those used hundreds of years ago for distribution all over the country.

It is an easy connection by boat from Kigoma town to Burundi and also down the length of Lake Tanganyika to Kasanga in Rukwa region and Mpulungu in Zambia.

After Jane Goodall published her research findings on Gombe Stream chimpanzees, great interest was kindled in these wonderful animals, particularly their ability to fashion and intelligently use simple tools. Kigoma town was the take-off point for Gombe Stream Game Reserve which became a National Park in 1968 and some individuals in the chimp community at Gombe became world celebrities.

From Kigoma, the more adventurous could also go to the Mahale Mountains National Park which lies to the south of Kigoma on the shores of Lake Tanganyika. Japanese scientists have worked at Mahale since the 1960s, researching and habituating the chimpanzees. Mahale also offers beautiful forest walks through an ornithologists' paradise, though the birds of Mahale have yet to be fully documented.

Playing host to refugees from neighbouring Rwanda, Burundi and the Democratic Republic of Congo (formerly Zaire) has, sadly, meant suffering for Kigoma and the Kagera region over the last few years. This large-scale human disaster has, as so often happens, taken its toll on the environment and the lives of local people. Tanzania should be recognised for the generous part it is playing in harbouring these suffering neighbours, even though in reality it cannot afford to do so.

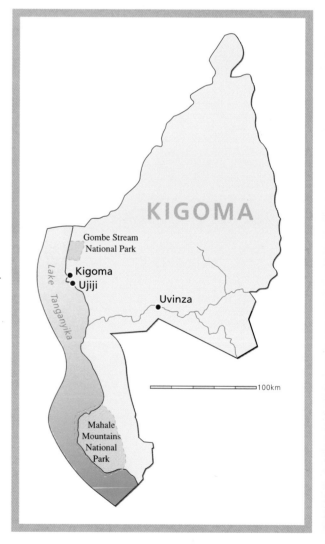

Around the bay from the centre of Kigoma town is Kibirizi. From here boats go up and down Lake Tanganyika. Boats are also made and fixed here. This huge canoe has probably had some maintenance done to it before it sets off again.

Kaunda Rokoba is a fisherman based in Kibirizi. He fishes *dagaa* during the night, mostly, and puts them out to dry in the morning. He has been fishing for 46 years.

The *MV Liemba* ferry anchored in the bay at Kigoma. The *MV Liemba* goes between Bujumbura in Burundi, Kigoma and Mpulungu in Zambia at the southern point of Lake Tanganyika. The *Liemba* is almost as old as the century. It was brought to the lake in bits on the railway. Hit by a bomb and then scuttled during World War I, she was salvaged in 1924. She was beached in 1970 and subsequently relaunched with new engines in 1979.

The boats anchored on the beach at Kibirizi are ready for whatever their cargo may be to whatever destination. Most of these boats will hop along the lake stopping at small villages along the way.

On Lumumba Road in Kigoma which descends down to the railway station and port, Ally holds fort in his restaurant. A very popular eating place in town, and rightly so.

Lumumba Road which goes through town is not unattractive due to the shady trees planted on either side.

Kigoma is very difficult to reach by road, like a few other major towns in Tanzania, so the rail links are vital for communication. The station in Kigoma was built in 1915 by the Germans when the railway line reached the lake.

Kigoma has a port which sends and receives goods from the neighbouring countries as well as Tanzania. From the port you can see the fuel tanks on the other side of the bay in Kibirizi.

The sun sets over the lake and a couple of canoes motor past…

This view of Lake Tanganyika from the road to Ujiji is quite different from the other parts of the lake. The Casvarina trees in the line by the water rather reminded me of Tuscany in Italy – though the palm trees in the foreground put paid to that. Lake Tanganyika is Africa's deepest lake at over 1400 metres and second largest lake at 675 km long and 50 km wide.

Shabani fixes inner tubes for a living in Ujiji, just south of Kigoma.

"Dr. Livingstone, I presume?" In Ujiji, on 10th November 1871 the erstwhile explorers Stanley and Livingstone met on this spot. Well that is what the plaque says, but as Philip Briggs tells us in his *Guide to Tanzania* "…All of which is rather poignant until you discover that Stanley's journal suggests the meeting took place near the old market several hundred metres from the monument…". I never knew that. He continues: "The probability is that when locals were quizzed by their German colonisers about where the famous meeting took place, they simply invented a plausible site - a scenario that will be familiar to anybody who has regularly asked for directions in Africa."

This is the museum at the site of the monument. The gentleman on the left in white is Henry Morton Stanley and on the right is Dr. Livingstone, captured in their moment of greeting. The illustrations around the walls will fill you in with any details on Stanley and Livingstone which you didn't know.

Gombe Stream National Park

Gombe Stream is the smallest of Tanzania's eleven National Parks. Without any roads, it is compact enough to be enjoyed on foot, and is more than beautiful enough to captivate the imagination of those who visit it. The Gombe Stream Game Reserve, as it was then known, was brought to public attention in 1960 by Jane Goodall, a British woman who initiated a fascinating study of wild chimpanzees. Gaining world-wide renown through Goodall's publications and Hugo van Lawick's photography, the Reserve was declared a National Park in 1968, and research into the habits of the chimpanzees continues to this day.

Gombe Stream National Park is bordered to the west by Lake Tanganyika which, sheltered in a trough of the Great Rift Valley, is the second deepest lake in the world, and the deepest and longest lake in Africa. It supports a spectacularly diverse fish population, parts of which can be viewed easily with a simple pair of water goggles. At certain times of the month, the activities of the Dagaa fishermen can also be watched, as they make camp on the shores of the lake and set out to fish as the sun goes down.

Moving away from the shores of the lake, and into the park's evergreen forest, one admires an intricate mass of plant and wildlife, whether it is the delicate beauty of the solitary butterfly or large groups of the chimpanzees and baboons. Because it drinks continuously from the waters of the stream, the forest is always verdant and teeming with life. It boasts many different mammals as diverse as the bushbaby, the porcupine, the mongoose and the bushpig, as well as several bird species, attracted by the abundance of its food and shelter.

Further north, the land becomes drier, and eventually gives way to grassland, a walk across which offers stunning views of the park and surrounding areas. Although chimpanzees are a little more likely to be seen in woodland areas, they can sometimes also be spotted in open land – of all large apes, they are the most adaptable. Chimpanzees make fascinating viewing, their distinctly individual characteristics and temperaments gradually becoming apparent. Living together in groups that vary in size from twenty to a hundred, you will always see them at Gombe Stream, and they certainly add to the unique magic of this tiny National Park.

Gombe Stream has a variety of vegetation types within its ecosystem, from dry forest to evergreen forest to woodlands and grasslands the higher you go. This is an example of the evergreen forest.

These chimpanzees, *Pan troglodytes schweinfurthii*, share 95% of our genes. In fact if you look at them there is bound to be someone you know recognisable in their faces or actions. This reclining lady is Fifi with little Frau behind her. Frau is about 9 mouths old and Fifi about 40 years old.

Scosha, 20 years old, with the most remarkable eyes. It is very uncommon to be able to see the whites of the eye on a chimpanzee, whereas on Scosha they give her a remarkably human look.

If there was ever a Godfather of Chimps, this is him: Gimbo, an 18-year-old male.

Kakombe Falls. A beautiful waterfall without a doubt, but beware! I left a jacket next to my seated guide and walked up to the waterfall to take some pictures. All's well at this point. Then I turned and ask the guide to shift a couple of metres with my jacket so I could shoot downstream. He couldn't hear me properly so got up and walked about 2 metres towards me, leaving the jacket on the log. Suddenly the jacket left the log and headed off into the bush. My jacket had been stolen by a baboon! We legged it into the bush chasing this demon but lost him, as well as my jacket which contained all the footage of the chimps and various bits of kit! After a long search – miracle of miracles – we found the jacket half buried in a pile of leaves surrounded by its contents. Much relieved, I got everything back except one film, number 6934. I hope he ate it and got indigestion! My guide said I was very lucky because the baboon was only half sized. Apparently a big one would have taken the jacket into a tree and that would have been that. Luck is relative I suppose.

The little lass at the bottom is Frau again; she will be breast-fed until she is about 2-2 $^{1}/_{2}$ years old.

Mahale Mountains National Park

Once in a while, I climb to one of the highest ridges in this park. Looking out through the forest canopy to the mountains in the west, rising behind. To the east I see the lake, more like a sea. I think of how it would be to walk over the thousand kilometres from Tanzania's coastline, across all that dry bush, then to climb these mountains through deep forest shadows, and finally rest the eyes on Lake Tanganyika. It appears like a miracle, acres of turquoise water glimpsed through lush vegetation, in the very heart of Africa.

150km down the eastern shores of this 700km long lake, we live on a forest island. Mountains rise up directly from the water to 2500m, their western slopes carpeted with rich semi-tropical gallery forest; all around, below, is the somewhat monotonous, dry bushland that covers most of western Tanzania. Within the bushland, this park is a haven of bio-diversity; its uniquely varied flora supporting a great range of fauna. For early man, it would have been the perfect land - water unlimited, shade and shelter under the trees, food in the forest.

Primates other than Man now dominate the forest, chimpanzees amongst them. Some days, I take visitors in to observe a group of wild-living chimpanzees that have been habituated for thirty years to human contact as part of a Japanese research project. We sit quietly as they eat, sleep, feed, fight, hunt and breed round us, bizarrely indifferent to our presence. We study these unspoilt cousins, in a daily life that mirrors man's, yet hasn't changed for millions of years.

Zoe Miller

The first European to discover the Mahale Mountains was V L Cameron when he arrived in Ras Kungwe on 23 March 1874. The next was Stanley who arrived two years later in 1876. The Mahale Mountains are a range of mountains reaching 2462m at their highest peak, Nkungwe. They jut out into Lake Tanganyika about 200km south of Kigoma almost exactly halfway down the lake. The mountains are home for a breath-taking diversity of wildlife and plantlife – a last bastion of true wilderness. They are extremely difficult to reach – by plane or boat – making the area particularly remote. The Government realised this and so, in 1985, the Mahale Mountains area, encompassing 1613 sq km, was gazetted as a National Park, thus preserving both the lives of many animals and the landscape. The park has no roads at all so the only way to see the park is by foot, enhancing the whole experience. It also made Mahale the first park in Tanzania's National Parks portfolio to be explored on foot.

As mentioned above, one of the park's special features is the huge primate population, especially chimpanzees. There are reckoned to be about 800-1000 chimps actually living in the park with a few small groups totalling about 80 which have been habituated and are fairly easy to see.

The most commonly seen group of chimps, 'M' Group, was habituated in 1968 at Kansanya by a method of habituating called 'provisioning' – providing food. The researchers would provide sugar cane and bananas mainly with some lemons, but also planted lemon trees which are now providing 'wild' food for the chimps. This 'provisioning' was drastically reduced in 1981 and by 1987 had been completely stopped, due to fear of the chimps becoming too used to people, running the risk of catching human diseases and being in danger from poachers. A human cold virus could kill a chimp.

The Mahale Mountains seen from Lake Tanganyika. In these mountains a vast range of animals, birds and plants are to be found and as yet still a wilderness. Mahale Mountains gets very few visitors making it probably one of my favourite parks – just you, the land and the animals.

The most efficient way of reaching Mahale Mountains is by plane. Of course you can reach Mahale by other means. For example, we drove from Moshi to Mpanda (3 full days). Then you drive another full day to reach Lake Tanganyika at about 4pm. If you are really lucky you can find someone who will rent you a boat and an outboard motor and will take you to the park. Remember, there has to be fuel for the motor – we were very lucky, there was. You have about a 3 hour boat ride down the lake to reach the camp HQ and then on again to the tented camp. An adventure and a miracle of logistics! Fly, if you can.

154

Mahale Mountains have a variety of wildlife. As I walked in the forest I saw bushbuck and various monkeys all still not used to humans, so even with my lightning fast reactions… I was unable to get a picture of them. But what you can be sure to see is chimpanzees. The chimps in these pictures are all from 'M' Group.

A small tree frog represents the reptiles in Mahale. There are plenty of snakes and lizards in and around the park – though I don't feel particularly strongly towards snakes.

The wildlife is more than just large mammals and birds – this butterfly, a Citrus swallowtail, *Papilio demodocus*, is one of the more common varieties in the park.

This young chimp is part of 'M' Group which has 30 chimps in it. He enjoys the lemons.

Chimps can get quite violent and sometimes make a hectic amount of noise. When running they can move very quickly over the ground, as he is doing here. Also they are not just vegetarians, they will occasionally attack and eat other monkeys. They did this at Mahale the day after I left – typical, they can be very inconsiderate sometimes.

A female eating lemons which are now wild but were planted in the 60s to aid research by 'provisioning', i.e. providing food for them so they are easier to get close to and study.

I think this chimp is Mkombo. Sometimes even the most detailed notes can fail you. If it is her, she is one of the older females in 'M'Group. Forgive me if I am wrong.

Kangwena Bay is the location for the super luxury tented camp I stayed at and this is their boat. There are few more beautiful and untouched places in Tanzania.

RUKWA

*T*ucked into the south-west corner of Tanzania, Rukwa region is one of the remotest in the country. With no rail links and roads which become difficult, as many, in the rainy season, it remains fairly isolated. The region offers a great deal to the curious traveller, from Lake Tanganyika and Lake Rukwa (from which the region gets its name) to Katavi Plains National Park. Apart from these natural areas there are the towns of Sumbawanga and Mpanda, both inimitable in their own ways.

One of the groups of people in Rukwa are the Fipa and in their language *Sumbawanga* means 'throw away your witchcraft'. Happily, the phrase has several different interpretations and one wonders whether the injunction to discard one's witchcraft is because of the Sumbawangan's aversion to sorcery or whether no-one can beat their witches, so better to 'throw away your witchcraft'.

Sumbawanga itself is a small but fast growing town with a large football stadium, probably built in anticipation of the population growth of the town. As is the case with most small towns, the people here are friendly and welcoming – any visitor will be immediately struck by their hospitality.

Mpanda, to the north of the region, is smaller than Sumbawanga, with dusty streets and a very relaxed atmosphere. Herer again the people show great hospitality and kindness and it is from Mpanda that you can drive to Lake Tanganyika in order to reach the Mahale Mountains National Park in Kigoma region. There is a very old town called Karema on the shores of Lake Tanganyika. Roman Catholic missionaries built a church there that would now be about a hundred years old.

Lake Tanganyika in the west of the region offers the visitor a plethora of different sights; from the large ferry going up to Kigoma or down to Zambia to the many small villages whose livelihood is dependant on fishing. The waters of the lake are crystal clear so any opportunity to go swimming with a mask should be taken to see the many different varieties of cichlid fish in the lake.

Lake Rukwa, on the other hand, is probably one of the shallower lakes in Africa – if shallowness can be defined – and in the dry season will split into two halves. Lake Rukwa also provides livelihoods for the local people by fishing. Around the lake, both in this region and Mbeya region, there is wildlife to be seen, although fairly scarce these days.

Another interesting physical feature in the very south-west of Rukwa region, on the Zambian border, is the Kalambo Falls. Wrapped in mystery and legend, Kalambo Falls is the second highest waterfall in Africa reaching an ethereal height of 215 metres.

North of Sumbawanga is Katavi Plains National Park which is perhaps the remotest and wildest National Park in Tanzania. This makes it for some people the ultimate safari destination. It teems with animals so your journey to get there is rewarded with a truly magnificent experience.

Altogether Rukwa region will give any visitor a feeling that they have really seen something special – the memory of it will last forever.

158

Early in the morning the sugar cane is prepared for a day in Mpanda's main market. Sugar cane is eaten as a thirst quencher and a sweet snack, full of sugar with no additives or preservatives. Very healthy, but bad for the teeth.

Even in Mpanda you will find a photo studio. This one is advertising that they take all kinds of pictures – passport, colour – fix broken cameras and develop colour films. Saatchi and Saatchi eat your hearts out.

159

A blue silk shirt and a dinner jacket are the uniforms of these lads hanging around outside an electrical shop in Mpanda. The people we met in Mpanda were extremely warm and welcoming and interested in who we were and what on earth we were doing there!

In the beginning God said …"and let there be light". Light transforming the ordinary into the extraordinary. A bicycle and a wall made into something soft and elegant when the truth is something commonplace.

160

Flying gives a very different perspective. This is the view of a couple of homes just outside Mpanda. The photographer is often the one to enjoy these images more because he will remember fondly leaning out of an empty door space in a very small plane and the pilot banking sharply so you can get a good angle…

Passing through Matai village we noticed this hotel with the amazing art painted on the outside. We came to the conclusion that the owners of this salubrious pad were fine philosophers, or if not philosophers then certainly very clever at encouraging people to eat without restraint.

Approaching Katavi Plains National Park from the south you will come across a small village called Usevya. This lorry is unloading all its goods for the monthly *mnada*. The *mnada* or 'auction' is the word used for market that happens once or twice a month. Throughout Tanzania almost every town and good-sized village will have a *mnada*. During most of the month the market space is empty but once or twice a month everyone piles in from all over the area to sell everything from fruit, vegetables, livestock and all kinds of hardware and other things you can see here. This truck had come from Sumbawanga in the south of the region.

Opposite: This region is a great producer of sunflowers. Usually the seed is crushed and used to make oil for sale on the local market. The residue, or cake, is used as animal feed.

162

Kalambo Falls, at 215 metres, is the second highest waterfall in Africa, surpassed only by the Victoria Falls. After a lengthy walk to the top, you wander around slightly nervously due to the precarious position you have to adopt to see the waterfall clearly. The Kalambo Falls are very near the border with Zambia.

"MBWILO"

There is a local legend about a snake called Mbwilo. This snake was about 4 metres long and amazingly multi-coloured, the likes of which had never been seen before and will probably never be seen again. The people who lived around here believed that it had special powers, so they tried to catch it. No-one ever did. Because of the special powers people believed it had, they would sacrifice animals over the Falls so that Mbwilo might heal a relative, or bring rain or help with food or any other basic human need. People believed strange miracles did happen and these were accredited to Mbwilo. But for many years now Mbwilo has not been seen and the practice of sacrificing animals over the falls has virtually ceased. The old people put it down to a lack of belief in the young people.

In Naopangala village on the shores of Lake Rukwa the houses of the fishermen and their families are basic and the vegetables provide a supplement to the diet of fish.

A wooden canoe pulled out of the water, a pair of '*thousand milers*' (the sandals made out of old tyres), the paddle and Lake Rukwa – some of the ingredients to life on the shores of Lake Rukwa, which legend has it is the shallowest lake of its size in Africa. In the dry season the lake divides into two, due to its shallowness. Some of the wide selection of fish they catch here are: *magege, kachinga, kambale, ningu, korokoro, matanta and kamdomo.*

Katavi Plains National Park

The park register of Katavi shows how rarely it is visited – no more than 50 times a year since its creation as a National Park in 1975; to the rest of the world Katavi is still a mystery.

Filling the floor of the Rukwa valley – a minor fault of the western rift – it spans over a million acres. From the escarpments fragile rivers run down through tamarind, fig and albida forests to feed vast seasonal floodplains. Across these plains run the last great herds of buffalo in East Africa – thick as bison in nineteenth century Kansas. Hippopotami mass along the creeks, grazing and sparring in the high heat of the day; elephant shake the fruit from the great borassus palms. This is truly the land of megaherbivores, a rare echo of the pleistocene drama played out in a landscape as yet untouched by the hand of man.

As always the seasons bring extraordinary change to the park. Only last year a terrible drought gripped the land, leaving the hippos confused and ankle deep in their own dung. I met crocodiles deep in the forest staggering towards some aardvark's hole for refuge; those that stayed on the river banks soon mummified with hollow gaping mouths. It seemed the land had died. And yet, as I write, two months of torrential rain have wrought an amazing transformation: Hippos porpoise in the current of once-dead rivers, buffalo stand in belly-high grass and families of elephant snorkel across the creek and into the blossoming trees. The dusty plain in front of camp is a lake once more and pygmy geese and gallinules busy along its shore.

So easy to imagine Katavi a as 'Lost World'; its boundaries have no fences, its animals defy the guidebooks on behaviour, human encroachment is unknown – although that will surely come. When the Tanzanian Government doubled the park's size in January 1997 to over 5,000 sq km it was an act of faith and daring. True wilderness has a value beyond the catchwords of conservation and development. Those few inspired travellers who walk through Katavi's plains and forests each year can feel it in their hearts core.

Roland Purcell

Katavi Plains at sunrise. When it first peeks over the horizon you are thinking to yourself "what is the day's new light going to bring?"... and then, "what on earth am I doing up at this time of day?"

Maasai giraffe are just one of the many species of animal you will see in Katavi.

The yellow-barked acacia tree, *Acacia xanthopholea*.

This is Lake Chada, or the remains of it. The whole area used to be under water with hundreds of crocodiles and hippos from horizon to horizon. Now it is drying up and there remains but a fraction of what was there previously. But the beauty is still there and the remoteness.

Each area of Katavi has distinct vegetation, leaving you with a different feel for each place. There are the huge expanses of empty grassland, the dried up lakes, forest area, rivers and an area like this; an area with dry, open and flat parts interspersed with trees and palms, which make for a very eerie feeling – particuarly if you are in the only vehicle in the park; the only visitor, just you and the animals. Katavi is definitely one of the best safari experiences I have ever had. The park is inimitable.

Opposite: This young lion is probably about a year old with faint remnants of his cub spots on his legs.

A flock of white pelicans, *Pelecanus onocrotalus*, fly past us. Katavi, because of the various rivers and ex-lakes, has many different water birds which come and go depending on the season and water levels.

A bow in the Kapapa River provides a home for hundreds of hippos. They naturally congregate in water to keep cool during the day, and leave the water to feed at night. Yet, ironically, they are not very sociable creatures and seem to bicker a lot when they are together in such numbers.

Overleaf: From the air an enormous herd of buffalo – could be a shoal of fish or swarm of ants with some imagination. Instead, it's a herd of one-ton beasts being followed by a flock of cattle egrets. The egrets are following the buffaloes to feed on the insects disturbed by the thundering herd.

Roan antelope, *Hippotragus equinus*, are rarely seen in the park. They are very shy and fly when they see you, so we were lucky. We had just spent an hour and a half driving down the wrong road to reach the camp at Ikuu. I think we had just stopped to stretch our legs and turn round and go back when we saw him!

This hippo at the front has been in a few scraps, not surprising when so many come together in one place.

MBEYA

Mbeya is a fairly mountainous region with the Uporoto and Rungwe mountain ranges which rise steeply in the east of the region (the Mtorwi and Rungwe peaks are 2,961m above sea level) then dip into Lake Nyasa in the south and to Lake Rukwa in the west. These extensive hills and mountains are what make up much of the southern highlands of Tanzania.

Mbeya is peopled by, among others, the Nyakyusa and the Safwa who originate from the mountains and the Nyika and Sangu who originally come from the plains.

Mbeya town itself sits between the Mbeya mountain range (Mbeya peak at 2,834m) and the Uporoto mountains at an altitude of 1,744m. Mbeya town is excellently connected to the rest of Tanzania and to Zambia and Malawi by good quality tarmac roads and the Tazara railway line has Mbeya as one of its biggest inland stations. The border town of Tunduma bustles with cross-border business and Tukuyu, south of Mbeya, which the Germans called Nieu Langenberg, is a pleasant little town tucked up in the mountains surrounded by tea plantations. Coffee is grown in the rest of the highlands of the region but has different seasons to the coffee grown in the north of the country.

Down on Lake Nyasa, whose tip only touches Mbeya region, one comes to Matema, well-known for its famous beach and beautiful scenery. It is at Matema that you can see lads surfing in their dug-outs or watch the fishermen out at night after the full moon. If you walk down the beach you can also see piles of beautifully made clay pots on sale on Saturday mornings.

West of Matema is Itungi, a port where one can travel by boat to Mbamba Bay – the southernmost port on Lake Nyasa – or to the various ports on the Malawi coast of Lake Nyasa. Kyela, near Itungi, grows what is said to be the tastiest rice in the whole of Tanzania.

The lowlands on the western part of Mbeya region are heavily cultivated with maize and other grain. The Usangu Flats are a fertile area producing rice, with the Mbarali Rice Scheme leading the production stakes. Mbeya shares the Ruaha National Park and the Rungwa and the Uwanda Game Reserves, but these are relatively small parts of the region. The magical Ngozi Crater Lake is situated high in the Uporoto mountains and is definitely worth a visit. The Mbozi meteorite is also worth looking at – an impressive looking boulder that fell from the sky many thousands of years ago. It is the third largest meteorite in the world. The other feature of the region that may be of interest to the visitor is 'Daraja la Mungu' which means 'Bridge of God'. It is a natural bridge formed over a river from cooled lava. Thus with its many diverse features Mbeya region offers both the visitor and resident a very special experience.

As the sun sets on the Mbeya range of hills behind Mbeya town, a crowd watch a football match.

Mbeya is the second biggest arabica coffee producing region in Tanzania and coffee shambas proliferate throughout the region. Coffee harvesting is done in certain seasons which differ from the north of the country to the south. This arabica cofffee is being harvested on Utengule Estate. The coffee from Mbeya region is ranked as some of the best in Tanzania and is popular in Germany. It is reckoned to be similar to Papua New Guinea's 'Y' Grade.

MBEYA

North of Mbeya about two hours is a small town called Chunya. In the 1920s and 1930s there was a massive gold rush to Chunya, but it petered out by the 1950s. After the gold Chunya became a tobacco centre. However this didn't last long and now the town is virtually empty, although there are still gold panners or miners at work in the area. We met Simon working in a dry river bed with his son. He told us that he had been panning in the area for about 50 years. For six months of the year he lives in the hills on a shamba where he farms in the wet season and in the dry season he comes down to pan for gold. He said the biggest piece of gold he had ever found was 40 grammes, about the size of an acorn. Chunya town is where he sells whatever he gets, which is enough to live on, he says. This picture shows Simon panning in the bottom of the hole they have been working on all day. They pan in the hole and also bring the dirt out of the hole, runing water over it to separate the mud, dirt and stones from anything that might be gold.

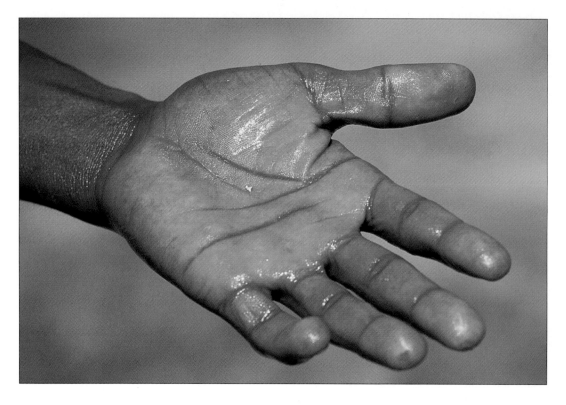

After a long days' work in the severely hot weather the rewards are like what you see here in the palm of his hand. This is not even enough to buy them both dinner.

The Mbozi Meteorite, which plummeted to earth many thousands of years ago, was first discovered by W H Nott, a private surveyor, in 1930. The meteorite weighs approximately 12 tons, is 1.22 metres high, 1.63 metres wide, 3.30 metres long and is technically termed 'medium octahedrite nickel iron' – in case you wanted to know. The meteorite is protected under the Antiquities Act of 1964 as there have been people who have tried to hack bits off it, so anyone trying that now – apart from the fact that the meteorite is extremely hard and virtually impossible to cut up – will get fined. Quite right.

Daraja la Mungu, or 'Bridge of God', across the Kiwira River is a natural rock bridge formed about 400 years ago from water-cooled lava which came from Mount Rungwe in the north-east.

Ngozi Crater Lake is situated in the Poroto Mountains. The lake is about 2 kilometres long and nestles in thick forest which is alive with the sounds of birds and other animals – great if you are an audiologist, but as they remain unseen, not ideal for the photographers of this world.

Matema is situated at the northernmost point of Lake Nyasa and is in the middle of a long and beautiful beach. The Livingstone Mountains meet the lake directly on the east side. Fishing is the main activity of the residents of the area. These gentlemen are fixing nets in readiness for their night's work.

Night fishing. The fishermen go out on a moonless night with bright lamps attached to the front of their boats to attract the fish. You can see the lights here with the spectacular back-drop of the Livingstone Mountains.

Opposite: The beach at Matema easily lends itself to rest and relaxation, with views over the lake and the mountains. You can hardly help yourself, trust me. The chair hints at someone's earlier contemplations and the fisherman returns home... life goes on... just.

Andrew, who, apart from weightlifting, greatly enjoys playing goalkeeper in the local football team, sits on the beach at Matema stretching and straining his enormous muscles. He asked me what kind of fitness regime I kept. After mumbling something pathetic about no opportunity because of travel, etc, etc, he laughed derisively and went back to lifting blocks of cement, explaining how vital exercise and big muscles were to one's good mental and physical health. I agreed with everything he said.

Every Saturday if you walk along the beach, past the mission, into Matema village you will find hundreds of clay pots like these for sale. They are all made locally and find their way all over Tanzania.

The lake and the mountains had an absolute grip on my thoughts and visions. At the end of the day the fishing is over and the hope is that there is enough to sell to buy whatever is needed, or even enough to feed everyone for dinner. They might catch *dagaa*, *mbasa*, *mbelele* or *ungosiola*.

SINGIDA

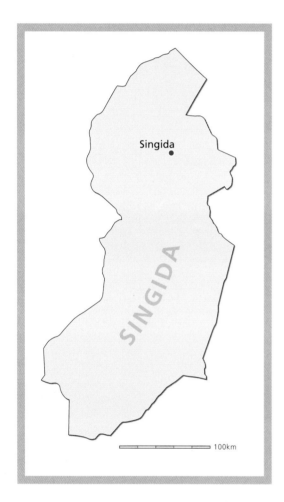

Singida is literally in the heart of Tanzania, and anywhere in the heart of a country the size and breadth of Tanzania is going to be difficult to reach. Singida, the town in the middle of the region, is just that. In the dry season you can reach town after many hours drive, whether from Dodoma, Arusha, Mwanza or Shinyanga. Each route will fill your car, eyes and lungs with dust and be incredibly hot. You may of course choose the wet season – your chances of arrival at Singida are drasti-

cally reduced but still possible (by helicopter). Anyway whether you arrive hot and dusty or covered from head to toe in mud probably having your car towed, you will never regret your arrival in Singida.

The region's centre is a pretty town which is littered with granite boulders in piles or kopjes, which gives it a unique setting. Having successfully reached it, a hint of temptation might creep in. Singida is not a rich region but the people are hard working, friendly and generous.

The main peoples found in the region are the Nyaturu and the Nyiramba – both of Bantu origins – and the Sandawe, who are one of the last Khoisan speakers left in east Africa. Today, if you venture down to Lake Eyasi in Arusha region, or into the north of this region, you might meet some of the Hadza people. They try as much as possible to retain their chosen life of hunting for meat and gathering from the forests and bush for whatever their needs may be. They have a greater knowledge of the bush than anyone is ever likely to learn in a lifetime's study and their respect for the land and the animals is second to none. We could learn a lot from these people were we to know it. Instead, like the Pygmy people in south-western Uganda and the Congo, they are just treated as tourist attractions. Their lifestyle changes and their hunting grounds shrink as the country is taken over by development and tourism. The traditional way of life of the Hadza or Sandawe may be soon gone.

The main occupation of the region is agriculture. The people grow mostly ground-nuts, pidgeon peas, castor oil plants, maize, millet and beans with a small amount of cotton, compared with the huge amounts grown in the neighbouring regions. The region is the country's biggest producer of ground-nuts, probably due to it's sandy soil being perfect for them to grow.

This part of Tanzania is well known for its cotton production. Most of the cotton is produced by the smallholder as a cash crop alongside food crops for subsistence. Finally black cotton soil lives up to its name.

As you approach Singida town you are met by this sign next to the boulders. A warm welcome indeed but still I am unable to translate the artistic graffiti. Any ideas on a postcard to…

All around Singida town you will find these very attractive piles of huge granite boulders which add an unusual flavour to the town, if maybe a slightly dusty one!

Sunset over Singida. On the right you can see Lake Singida, an important lake for water birds in this arid area.

A young lady peers into a small duka, or shop, in town. These small shops sell a vast array of different items: from flip-flops to radios and toy mobile phones to flour and beans.

DODOMA

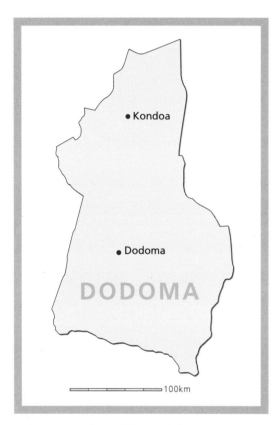

is not well provided with road or railway links to the rest of the country. Today, the Government's commitment to move to Dodoma is more in word than in deed. Most sessions of the Tanzanian Parliament take place in Dodoma, the longest being the Budget Session. Immediately before it all the senior government officials and their Ministers move to Dodoma and no sooner has the session ended than everybody packs the files and moves back to Dar es Salaam.

Admittedly, the twenty-five years of fading commitment to 'move to Dodoma' has transformed Dodoma from being a dusty, nondescript railway station town in the middle of an arid land to a green municipality with brisk business that gets even brisker during parliamentary sessions. The Gogo people, who would probably have been forgotten and marginalised in an infrequently visited region, have taken advantage of the capital, and the politicians who frequent the town, to make themselves heard and to advance their interests.

The Gogo are pastoralists and agriculturalists and over and above the normal cultivation of maize, millet and beans a new crop has been introduced to Dodoma – grapes. Dodoma's vineyards will not compete with France's best but it is a brave beginning and a promising one. Dodoma's red port (temporarily out of production) is considered one of the most potent wines of its kind.

North of Dodoma is Kondoa where the Irangi people live. Kondoa is famous for its historic rock paintings – mainly around Kolo, a small trading centre 22km north of Kondoa. There are over 100 known sites

here and the paintings which go back 4,000 years, depict animals such as giraffe, antelope and eland. Some show activities that resemble religious ceremonies while others are abstract geometric figures. The identity of the painters and the meaning of the paintings – excluding the purely aesthetic pleasures of creating art – is still the subject of conjecture.

When Tanzania's government and the then ruling party, TANU, vowed to move the country's capital from Dar es Salaam to Dodoma, the choice was more political than practical. True, Dodoma, geographically in the centre of the country, was acceptable to both Moslems and Christians and in its elevation to capital of Tanzania was believed to uplift the lives of the Gogo people who live around the town. However, Dodoma is semi-desert, with a growing shortage of water. Apart from the central railway-line and the tarmac road to Dar es Salaam via Morogoro – built after the decision to move the capital was made in October 1973 – Dodoma itself

The Kolo or Irangi Rock Paintings found near Kolo village on the main road from Arusha due south to Dodoma. These are ancient cave paintings dating back from 3500 BC to 600-800 AD There are three sites of paintings at Kolo, this site's paintings, in dark red, open to the elements as Mother Nature intended, show that these paintings of people and animals, in particular the giraffe, date back to 3500 BC. If you reach Kolo, ask Juma Mpore, the guide, to tell you his story of when Mary Leakey came here to age the paintings, 30 years ago.

The bus station in Kondoa in the north of the region. Travelling by bus in Tanzania is a great experience, like the most exciting roller-coaster ride, but without seat belts.

Second-hand clothes are big business throughout the country. This chap is selling T-shirts and shorts in Kondoa. (Near the bus station, in case you see anything you like.)

On Kondoa's main street the wholesaler has his goods on the side of the road. He seems to specialise in soap and oil.

In the middle of a maize field, just north of Dodoma, a wind-powered water pump makes sure the crops are kept irrigated, as this part of the country is very dry and hot. Which I found out when I had to walk a few kilometres with my cameras after having been arrested by an army corporal – the charge being photographing in an army area. The problem was that the 'Do not photograph because you are in an army area' sign was 100% covered by bushes and trees and totally invisible. Eventually we sorted the problem out very amicably.

Dodoma airport with Simba Rock overlooking it.

In the main market in Dodoma town Bakari Salim is selling coconuts brought up from the coast. Most likely from Dar as there is a tarmac road all the way.

In the market various food is available to supply nourishment for the energetic shoppers and sellers. This is the chapati centre. The chefs are often complaining about the strict health standards under which they have to try and operate…

Dodoma railway station at the end of a hectic day feels very calming. The trains taking passengers and freight go through Dodoma on the way to Tabora, Mwanza, Kigoma and Dar es Salaam.

Straight Road in Dodoma.

About 30 kms south-east of Dodoma is the Mvumi hospital. Mvumi was established as a hospital in 1934 – there was a dispensary before-hand – under the Anglican Diocese of Central Tanganyika. The hospital has developed, over the years, its eye department. Today people will travel from all over Tanzania and the neighbouring countries to have their eyes fixed. There were two eye surgeons at work in the theatre when I went in: Dr. Marilyn Scudder and Dr. Isseme. This is Dr. Isseme operating on a patient's eye. I am not the most squeamish person so I could deal with it. What shook me was when Dr. Isseme finished the operation on this eye, he said, "OK, you can go now," and the patient got up and walked out. His eye had been under local anaesthetic and so he had been totally conscious throughout the whole ordeal. Quite normal practice with eye ops, I gather. Eagh.

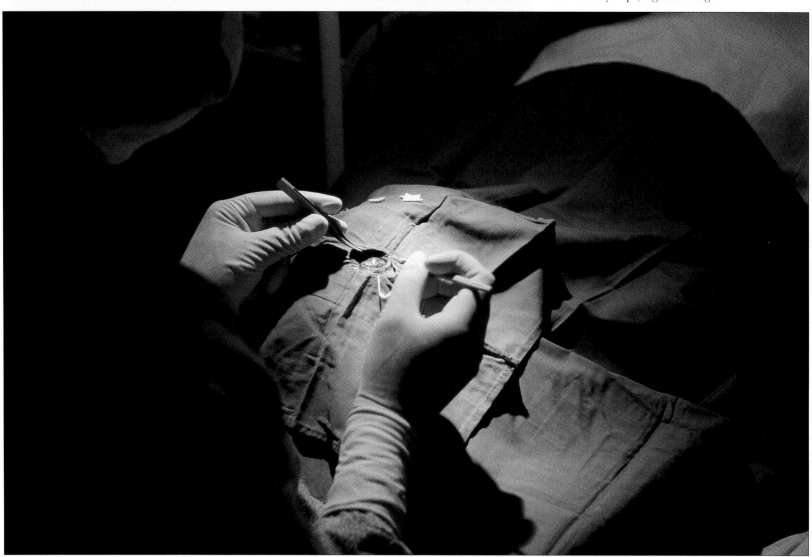

The houses in Dodoma region often have flat roofs, which are useful for drying crops because it rarely rains. The wooden tools lying in front of the house are for crushing dried maize to make flour to mix with water to make *ugali*, a staple food.

IRINGA

The people who dominate Iringa region are today known as the Hehe. The name derived from Europeans visiting the area in the nineteenth century who heard their battle cries of "Hee, hee, hee." In those days the region was dominated not by one group of people but by various groups from Usagara, Ubena and Ukimbu. They were brought together by Munyigumba, who came to power in 1855. By strength of character and military ability he united the people and established a large chiefdom at Rungemba. When he died in 1878, his son, Mkwawa, took over and expanded the Hehe territory even further. It was Mkwawa who gave the Germans the hardest time establishing colonial rule in the country. Although finally defeated, he chose suicide rather than suffer the disgrace of capture. Apart from the Hehe, Iringa's people include the Kinga and the Bena. The Kinga are known for their business acumen, not unlike the Chaggas of Kilimanjaro.

Today, Iringa, with an altitude of 1,582m, is a thriving town with a very pleasant climate and friendly people. One reaches Iringa by road from Dodoma or Dar es Salaam and the road goes on to Mbeya or Songea. The Tazara railway-line has a station at Makumbako, a bustling and fast growing town on the road from Dar es Salaam, and through Iringa to Mbeya and on into Zambia passes through Makumbako.

Most of the region is mountainous and so Iringa is the country's biggest producer of tea, which is grown in the spectacularly beautiful highlands of Mufindi as well as slightly lower down at Njombe. Pyrethrum, whose flowers produce a natural insecticide, is also grown in the Mufindi, Njombe and Makete districts of Iringa. Wattle, which produces tannin, abounds in Njombe where there is a wattle extract factory. The Mufindi pulp and paper factory uses the vast softwood forests, planted for the purpose, to produce most of Tanzania's paper. On the agricultural side, Iringa produces potatoes and wheat on the highlands and maize, beans and rice in the lowlands. The Dabaga factory, just outside Iringa town, processes Iringa's excellent fruit and vegetables to make bottled ketchup – probably the best ketchup in East Africa – as well as various other pickles and preserves.

For the visitor, Ruaha National Park is normally easily accessible from Iringa town. The park has stunning scenery which is divided by the Great Ruaha River and the park has a huge population of wildlife of great diversity. Another feature of the region are the Livingstone Mountains in the south-west on the edge of Lake Nyasa. For the adventurous walker it would be a marvellous experience to cross the mountains and end up at the lake.

Mufindi, in the highlands of the region, south-west of Iringa town, is one of the main centres for tea in Tanzania. Brooke Bond has been farming tea in this area since 1941, when it was invited in by the custodian of enemy property to manage the tea farms of interned Germans. After the war the company was given the opportunity to purchase most of the land and properties from the custodian, which it did. It has farmed here ever since.

A tea nursery with a variety of clonal tea bushes, selected for their various desired qualities.

To reach export readiness tea has to go through many processes – like most commodities. This is the CTC machine, Cutting, Tearing and Curling machine, which shreds the tea leaves.

The tea ferments in these containers for about one hour. Warm air is passed through the bottom and a careful eye is kept on the temperature, by the thermometer stuck in the middle. After the tea has been in here for an hour it will go through the CTC machine again and then be fermented for another hour before moving onto the drying machine, where the fermenting process is stopped.

The final process in a long line: packing. The tea has been cut, fermented, dried, sorted and eventually reaches the packing machines. The tea comes out of the white funnels and is packed tightly into the paper packets. From here it will be exported, much of it to Pakistan.

The main street in Iringa.

At Don Bosco's Youth Training Centre in Iringa, Constantino welds back a broken spring bracket on some very poor soul's damaged Landrover… All over Tanzania you can find Don Bosco's Youth Training Centres set up by a Catholic monk called Don Bosco who had a heart for young people and trade. They are centres where young people are trained in all types of skills, such as: mechanics, welding, carpentry, printing, plumbing, electrical engineering among others.

In Makambako, a junction in the main road from Dar to Mbeya, you will find a petrol station, a couple of places to eat and the opportunity to gamble your blues away. This highly complex game is a cross between poker, chess, backgammon, dice, snakes and ladders and any other kind of game you like to mention. Watching the game for a while, I felt sure I understood how to play. The big mistake was asking someone the rules – total confusion!

South of Iringa town you will find the Isimilia Stone Age Site, first excavated by Professor Howell of Chicago University in 1957. At the site is a small museum which houses various items, including tools and weapons. These sandstone pillars, along a gully from the site, were formed by a river long dried up.

Ruaha National Park

One of East Africa's most renowned areas of wilderness, and the second biggest of its National Parks, Ruaha, untouched by human habitation, has a very distinctive atmosphere. It boasts a great diversity of landscapes and wildlife and, situated in the very heart of Tanzania, its appeal is intensified by its remote position.

The name 'Ruaha' is derived from the Hehe people's word iuvaha, which means 'stream, river or brook'. The real name of this Iuvaha river, which passes through the park, is 'Lyambangari', and the valleys which surround this and other rivers in Ruaha support a great variety of animal life and vegetation. Perhaps the most extraordinary of the rivers in Ruaha are the Mwagusi and the Mdonya Sand rivers, which are, for most of the year, streams of sand, supported by natural underground water supplies. However, after the rains, they are filled by surging water, transforming, for a time, the landscape of the park. Around the Mwagusi river in particular, buffaloes are often spotted, along with the elegant giraffe, attracted by the lush vegetation surrounding the water. Prides of lions are also found in this area, and can often be seen resting during the day.

The Makeluga and Ruaha rivers, beautiful in their own terms, are also worth visiting for the many animals which gather along their shores. The very fortunate visitor may catch a glimpse of the magnificent sable antelope looking for food during the dry season. But otherwise there is still more than enough wildlife to view. The plains which border the rivers are often home to two of East Africa's most graceful animals: the cheetah and the impala, the latter often the prey of the former. The zebra frequents this area of the park, as does the ostrich and the long-crested eagle.

Ruaha is also home to the largest population of elephants in any of Tanzania's National Parks. However, it is not only the diverse animal life which makes Ruaha such a fascinating place to visit. The variety of vegetation and landscapes, ranging from the aforementioned sand rivers to the beautiful Nyamakuyu rapids, and from endless grassy plains to dense and lush woodland, gives Ruaha a very special character.

Ruaha National Park is named after the Great Ruaha River, seen here diminished from its former glory by very low water levels. A whole ecosystem depends on this river, which flows right through the park.

A young female Greater kudu, *Tragelaphus strepsiceros*. The park has both the Greater and Lesser kudus, the distinguishing features being that the Lesser are smaller, with smaller horns, and have two conspicuous white patches on the upper and lower parts of the neck.

The park also has grassy plains contrasting with the forest and bush that flourishes along the river. The hill in the distance is Chiriwindi Hill.

The Silver or Black-backed jackal, a monogomous creature, is mainly a scavenger, eating rodents and insects
and occasionally stealing new-born gazelle fawns.

The Great Ruaha River provides food for many animals and reptiles.
This elephant has enjoyed the bathing potential of the river and is currently feasting on the fresh grass which is constantly irrigated by the river.

Burchell's zebra, *Equus burchelli* (which sounds more like an opera than the scientific name for a zebra), seen near Kimiramatonge Hill.

The area in the north of the park along the Mwagusi Sand River has another type of land-scape full of Doum palms. The Mwagusi was also at the time very low, so you could see where elephants had walked into the sandy river bed, digging for water.

A pair of lions struggle through another day of gruelling toil near the Great Ruaha River.

This Baobab tree has been used as a scratching post by elephants; you can see the bark worn off on the trunk.

Udzungwa Mountains National Park

This park is very new to the National Parks portfolio; established in 1993 it is still in its early years. Yet despite this it shows signs of being one of the gems. Udzungwa Mountains National Park spans an area of about 1,000 square kilometres and has a huge altitude range from 300m to 2800m above sea level. The park is based around the Udzungwa Mountains whose northerly boundary hosts the Great Ruaha river and eastern boundary the road to Ifakara. The park has great biodiversity; from the forest which climbs from 300m upwards to the open grasslands in the western part of the park. The forest has many special features, from the amazing plantlife to the extensive birdlife and animals. One particular feature is the endemic primates of Udzungwa: the Iringa red colobus monkey and the Sanje mangabey. The former is more easily seen although still shy and high up in the trees and the latter is quite rare. The other primates of the park include Vervet monkey, the ubiquitous baboon, Syke's monkey and the Black-and-white colobus.

A couple of days walk from the headquarters, in the western part of the park, you will find areas of open grassland where many larger mammals live, such as elephant, buffalo, lion, leopard, sable, eland, duiker and bushbuck. These are not easy to see as the area has only recently become protected so the animals are still very wary.

The forest has various streams and rivers running through it, the biggest being the Great Ruaha river on the northern boundary, but there are also small rivers, which make another special feature of the park, and the Sanje waterfalls. This is a series of small waterfalls with a large one at the end, which plummets over a cliff-face to make the whole area particularly picturesque.

The park has always been a major natural resource for the people of the area, in particular for firewood, and so the park has several projects working with the local community so that they too can benefit. The main work being done by the park is the growing of tree seedlings for free distribution to the villages of the area. This will hopefully over time cease the necessity of the people to collect firewood from the park – thus keeping the area fully protected.

Udzungwa Mountains National Park still has very few visitors, yet for anyone interested in birds and plants and for anyone who likes quiet walks through undisturbed forest and grassland and to those who can't live without camping in the bush and being completely self-sufficient, then this is definitely a park not to be missed.

The park is working very closely with the local people so that the conflict of interests is kept to an absolute minimum. Conflict can occasionally arise when people are suddenly denied access to a major resource, i.e. wood in the National Park. Fortunately, the park authorities are working on this issue very carefully. Firstly, they are slowly phasing out wood collection as opposed to an immediate ban, and secondly, they have an enormous tree nursery project. These are fast growing exotic hard-wood seedlings, *Cedrela odorata*.

Udzungwa, Tanzania's newest national park, is aimed at conservation of the forest and its animals and resources. Also how the park affects the people of the area and the resulting conflicts and resolutions. Definitely the way forward.

These seedlings are given out to the local people free to encourage planting and to help sustain people who have survived for years on the wood from the Udzungwa Mountains. The park has seven tree nurseries to help the people in this way.

The Sanje Falls has three smaller falls above it; as far as I could gather they were called Falls 1, Falls 2 and Falls 3. This is Falls 2.

The forest is a mass of vegetation, wildlife and birdlife; most of the animals are still very shy, not yet used to people, but you hear a great deal. In the early 1980s there was a special scientific discovery of a monkey, the Crested Mangabey. Following this discovery many other new biological discoveries were made. This slightly peculiar tree is *Casia excelsa*.

The main Sanje Falls which drops a magnificent 170 metres to the valley below. The river which flows through the park is very likely to be a tributary of the Great Ruaha River.

The sun sets behind the Udzungwa Mountains.

MOROGORO

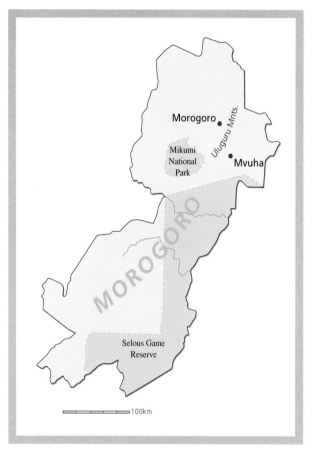

Morogoro is a green, fertile region that borders what is considered the 'north' (Arusha) as well as what is considered the 'south' (Lindi and Ruvuma). It also borders the coast regions to the east, which people of Morogoro town describe endearingly as *mji kasoro bahari* (the town that misses the sea).

Morogoro town itself, although small and rather old fashioned, hums with life. All the traffic that goes to Dodoma, Tanzania's political capital city, from Dar es Salaam, Tanzania's commercial and de facto capital city, must pass through Morogoro and more often than not, fill up their motor vehicles and take a meal in Morogoro's numerous popular restaurants. The heavy trucks that go to the southern regions of Mbeya, Iringa and Ruvuma and often cross Tanzania to Zambia, Malawi and Southern Congo from the port of Dar es Salaam – or the other way round – pass through Morogoro and their drivers will buy fruit and foodstuffs which abound in the many markets in and around the town.

Although Dar es Salaam may have the sea, Morogoro is one of the greenest towns in Tanzania, and trees of all kinds line its streets. The several factories that at one time had stopped working are now in the process of being privatized and revived. The Moproco oil and soap factory is now in full production and so is the canvas factory.

Morogoro is the land of the Luguru, Sagara, Pogoro, Kutu, Kaguru, Nguu and the Mbunga people. It was the Mbunga people that ignited the Maji Maji uprising in 1905. The Mbunga are actually a faction of the Nguni people who had fled from the Zulu wars of the great King Shaka. There is no doubt the Mbunga harnessed the military skills started by Shaka in fighting the Germans so successfully in the early days of the uprising.

Coffee and sisal are the region's two major cash crops. Pyrethrum was also grown in the Uluguru highlands. Down in the valleys of the Ruaha, Rufiji and Wami rivers and in the fertile Kilombero valley maize, millet, rice, vegetables, fruit and sugar cane are grown in great abundance. Two sugar factories have been built in the Kilombero

valley and another at Mtibwa near Turiani.

Excellent quality rubies are mined in the Uluguru mountains and mica is so plentiful in Morogoro that one of its districts has been given the Swahili word for mica: *Ulanga*.

Morogoro region shares almost half the Selous Game Reserve, but it is the Mikumi National Park that is its real pride. Any traveller to the south of Tanzania from Dar es Salaam, whether by road or the Tazara train, will pass through this small but very full national park and, often and unexpectedly, a giraffe will come loping across the road or a heard of zebras will be seen nibbling the grass growing beside the railway. Take care because here, animals have the right of way!

Opposite: Morogoro town is at the centre of a major agricultural area and is pleasantly located at the foot of the Uluguru Mountains.

Chinga Boy, third from left in the Muslim cap, is the enterprising chap who takes his travelling HMV around town, playing the music he sells. Clever principle really, if you are interested in buying one of his tapes but aren't sure what the artist sounds like, he'll put it on for you and everyone for hundreds of yards around to hear.

By the addition of a few trees many years ago the centre of Morogoro was transformed into the pleasant place it is today.

With the Uluguru Mountains as a backdrop, Jijiga, in the red, play Burkina in the green. A local league game with both sides coming from the same area of town. Football is the main sport of Tanzania and has a great following at every level. Jijiga won.

Most bricks in Tanzania are made like this on the local level. The clay is dug from the ground, moulded into brick shapes and left to dry in the sun for 4 days; once dry they are stacked into piles and left for another week. Finally the bricks are made into their own kiln, fire is put underneath and they are cooked for about 4 days — and, voila, a massive stack of very useful bricks.

217

The main piece of machinery needed to process sisal is this Decorticator. This machine removes the green skin of the sisal and reveals the fresh sisal at the end ready for the next step. This particular example had temporarily ceased to function but was to be repaired imminently.

Opposite: Sisal is one of the major agricultural activities in the region. The sisal is harvested, laid out in bundles (as seen here) and then piled into blocks before being collected by truck and taken to the factory. One of the cutters told us that harvesting sisal was alright but you do get problems with snakes (in particular cobras), rats, lizards and the very sharp and hard points of the sisal itself.

The now skinless and wet sisal is transported outside where it dries in the sun on special racks for about 6 to 10 hours depending on the weather.

After the sisal has dried, it is brought to the Brushing machine where it is smoothened and strengthened. Sisal is mainly exported from Tanzania to China, Europe and the United States with a small amount remaining in Tanzania.

When you cross the Uluguru Mountains heading south, you will come to a small village called Mvuha. In this village is a unique chemist. *Duka la madawa* means chemist.

Sisal is used to make rope, string and mats. One of the local uses for processed sisal is the making of mattresses. Here the lads can be seen stuffing sisal into mattresses on the side of the road in Morogoro. Another local use for sisal is coffee export bags which are woven in mills in Moshi and Morogoro.

Selous Game Reserve

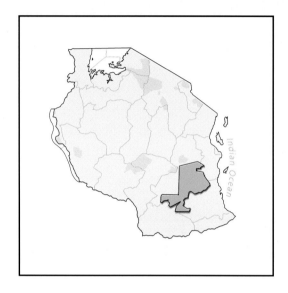

The Selous Game Reserve, situated towards the south of Tanzania, stretches to 50,000 sq km. It is the biggest natural protected area in East Africa.

Selous possesses a history both interesting and varied. It was, in the past, on the trade routes which passed from the heart of the country to the coast and was traversed by several European explorers in the nineteenth century. However, during the First World War, Selous was a battlefield, and the Reserve actually takes its name from the British explorer, Frederick Courteney Selous, who was killed there during the war and after whom the famous Selous Scouts were named.

In 1982, the United Nations heralded the Selous Game Reserve as a 'World Heritage Site'. Yet, despite this honour, the Reserve is by no means always engulfed by tourists, which allows those who do choose to visit it a particularly peaceful and stimulating experience. The environments of the Selous are many and varied; perhaps the most imaginative way to enjoy some of the Reserve's natural wonders is to take a boat down the Rufiji river, or even a twelve-day river rafting safari. From this mobile vantage point, visitors are able to observe the activities of wildlife such as hippos, buffalo, waterbuck and crocodiles.

However, to catch a glimpse of the Reserve's most spectacular wildlife one must venture into the wilderness of Selous, where the animal population of East Africa can be enjoyed in all its natural beauty. Every visitor longs to see the lions, which are, of course, spectacular, but the persistent may also be rewarded with a sighting of a leopard or, on extremely rare occasions, a cheetah. Particularly famous for its elephants, Selous also boasts a large population of hippos and a dwindling number of black rhinos – dwindling because of poaching.

Spectacular for their sheer numbers are Selous's herds of buffaloes, especially for those who are fortunate enough to see them come in their hundreds to drink at the Rufiji river. Also extraordinary in their elegance are Selous's breeds of antelope: the impala, the sable antelope, the Greater kudu, the eland, the wildebeest and the hartebeest – a collection whose sheer diversity reflects the wealth and abundance of the Reserve's animal kingdom.

223

The Rufiji River is a dominant feature of the Selous Game Reserve in the northern sector and much of the game congregates around the river. Occasionally, if you are lucky, you see elephants crossing a river. They can swim out of their depth using their trunks like snorkels to breathe.

224

This hippo skull on the banks of the Rufiji River shows what enormous tusks they have.
These are only used for fighting and displays of strength as hippos are herbivores.

A yellow-billed stork, *Mycteria ibis*, on the edge of the river. Storks eat small fish, grubs and bugs found in the shallows.

This baby crocodile, weeks old and still the size of a lizard, already feeds on small fish.

The Rufiji river has an abundance of crocodiles on its shores. The sex of crocodiles is determined by sand temperature in which the eggs are laid. Hot sand will produce females and cool sand will produce males. Whether or not this determines their characters has yet to be established.

The banks of the Rufiji River are lined with
Borassus palms, *Borassus aethiopum*, the fruit of
which is very popular with elephants, who help
to distribute them via their dung.

This Baobab tree, hundreds of years old, is sometimes called the 'upside down tree' as the whole tree looks as if it has been planted the wrong way up, with the roots pointing skywards.

Cattle egrets, *Ardeola ibis*, are a common sight on the banks of the Rufiji.

This Little bee-eater, *Merops pusillus*, was a loyal guard at Frederick Courteney Selous's grave near Beho Beho.

The African wild dog, the most amazing of all African animals, is reasonably common in
the Selous, where research is being carried out on it. People think that the species found in
the Selous is slightly different to that found in the north of Tanzania. You can imagine my
excitement when I finally saw a wild dog in the wild.

The wildebeest found in the Selous are a different type to those of the northern parks of Tanzania. These are Blue wildebeest or Brindled gnus as opposed to the Common wildebeest or White-bearded gnu. These fellows lack the white hair hanging down from their chins and their coats are lighter in colour.

The top of the springs at Beho Beho. The water is hot and sulphurous, flowing down towards the middle of the picture where it falls over a small drop and collects in pools. It is rumoured that these springs could have been the source of the magic water which was used in the Maji Maji rebellion (see Introduction).

Two young female Defassa waterbucks, *Kobus defassa*. They will lose the blow-dried look as they get older.

The Monitor lizard can reach an enormous size and fully-grown ones can easily be mistaken for crocodiles, well… at a very quick glance anyway.

The sunsets in the Selous are stunning. The Rufiji River and Borassus palms.

Mikumi National Park

Lying just to the north of the Selous Game Reserve, Mikumi National Park is the third largest of Tanzania's parks. It stands in the Mkata flood plain, and is bordered to the east by the Uluguru Mountains and to the west by the Rubeho Mountains. In 1954, the completion of the road which links Morogoro with Iringa gave rise to an influx of hunters whose activities greatly threatened the stability of the animal population in this part of Tanzania. It was in response to threats such as this that the Mikumi National Park was established in 1964, with extensions added in 1975.

The Mkata flood plain itself has many varieties of animal, and Kikoboga, in the south of the plain, is particularly notable for its yellow baboons — lighter in colour and size than those found in other parts of Tanzania. Also there are African elephants and herds of graceful eland and hartebeest and sometimes the visitor may be lucky enough to catch sight of the Greater kudu, a rather beautiful type of large antelope.

Following the Mkata river to the north, one passes through areas of swamp where buffaloes and warthogs are often sighted — and also occasionally the rather conspicuous saddle-billed stork, whose white body and red and black bill, complemented by a yellow 'saddle', deserves more than a second glance. The hammer-headed stork, whose name accurately sums up its curious physical appearance, may also be seen in swampy districts during the journey north.

Further north, towards Mwanambogo, are prides of lions, which actually live throughout the expanse of the flood plain. The lions' main prey in Mikumi is the wildebeest, and in particular the Blue wildebeest (also known as the Brindled gnu), which is especially common in this area. The most keenly observant may also be fortunate enough to spot, in this area, the python, a vicious, although non-poisonous, snake which can grow to as large as six metres.

Turning right to the south of this large park, in Ikoya, which lies beside the Mkata river, leopards can very occasionally be seen lounging in the trees — though as they are generally nocturnal animals, sightings are rare. Much more easily spotted are zebras and the ever graceful giraffe. If one is able to visit the southern extension of the park, which is not yet fully developed for tourism, the beautiful sable antelope is another attraction.

234

Mikumi, unlike any other national park, has a major tarmac road cutting straight through the middle of it. The main road from Mbeya to Dar es Salaam hammers through endangering the wildlife, thus the huge signs. Other parks, such as the Serengeti and Katavi Plains, have public roads running through, but they are dirt roads which tends to slow drivers down.

Burchell's zebra venture bravely onto the main road going through the park. Because it is a tarmac road, people travel very quickly and so animals like these, especially at night, haven't a hope. On the other hand it makes Mikumi the most accessible National Park to Dar es Salaam, an easy 3 to 4 hours drive.

In the Ikoya area south of the main road we found this beautiful lioness. Lions are incredibly relaxed creatures; they spend the vast majority of the day sleeping. Then the lionesses may try to hunt, often unsuccessfully. If they succeed, they gorge themselves and then sleep again. The big-maned male will rarely join in the hunting but will more than likely demand first portion of the killed prey, and will only let the hunters in when he can hardly eat any more. 'King of the Jungle' – they don't even live in the jungle.

Two female impalas, *Aepyceros melampus*, the one on the left showing a typical pre-flight alertness. These two would be part of a breeding herd which is shepherded around by one territorial male.

A pair of Yellow-billed storks, fishing in Mwanambogo Dam, in the northern part of the park.

This hippo pool is completely covered by Nile cabbage, a serious weed threatening many pools, lakes, dams and waterways in Africa. Here you can see bits of hippos and a hippo exhaling from his or her nose. One way of distinguishing hippo sexes is that the male hippo ears stand more vertical and his neck is bigger.

237

Male elephants will often become solitary or spend time with one or a few other older males, only occasionally meeting cow herds but never staying for long.

A view of the park across the Mkata Flood Plain.

Maasai giraffe in the Ikoya section of the park. Each giraffe has individual markings and despite its very long neck has only 7 vertebrae, like humans.

RUVUMA

Ruvuma region is named after the Ruvuma river which virtually forms the southern border of Tanzania. Ruvuma's capital is Songea reached by an excellently constructed tarmac road from Iringa past Makambako and Njombe or by another road, which is difficult during the rainy season, from Mtwara and Lindi. Lake Nyasa borders Ruvuma region in the west and the fertile and intensively cultivated Matengo highlands rise from the lacustrine lowlands.

It is here that coffee is grown in great abundance. These highlands are peopled by the Matengo, who are said to have been driven up there by the warlike Ngoni as they escaped from the Zulu struggles in South Africa in the mid-1800s. The Matengo have, traditionally, been great soil conservationists, and their unique *vinyungu* system of agriculture involves digging depressions on hill-sides and cultivating crops in the resulting depressions without causing soil erosion or loss of fertility.

Immediate neighbours of the Matengo are the Nyasa people. As the name may suggest, these people gave their name to the lake, and they inhabit Malawi as well as Tanzania. The Nyasa are excellent fishermen and Lake Nyasa provides rich fishing waters. The lake itself it unique in that it has the greatest number of indigenous fish of all the fresh water lakes in the world.

Around Songea town, the Ngoni people live and carry on their farming business. Ruvuma region is famous for maize and tobacco is also grown with much success. The Ngoni-Matengo Co-operative Marketing Union, popularly known as the 'Ngomat', was formed in 1936 with the main object of marketing fire-cure tobacco produced in what is now Ruvuma region.

The south-east of Ruvuma region is the land of the Yao. The Yao, like the Nyamwezi in Tabora and the Kamba in Kenya were intrepid long-distance traders. As early as the 16th century, the Yao were trading iron hoes and implements made by themselves for salt, livestock, food and skins. With the coming of Arab traders and slavers and the upheaval that followed the Ngoni invasion in the mid-

1800s, the Yao, under powerful leaders such as Mpanda, Mataka, Machemba and Mtalika, got more and more involved with the slave trade and guns, cloth, beads, glass and various trinkets were exchanged for slaves. Today, the land of the Yao, on the banks of the Ruvuma river, is a potentially lucrative gemstone mining area. Since the early nineties, hundreds of young Tanzanian fortune seekers have gone to Tunduru to dig up the muddy banks of the Ruvuma looking for such precious stones as diamonds and alexandrine. A few have struck it lucky and many more persevere.

Songea town in the heart of the region is a small but lively place which features the Maji Maji Memorial. This is a monument and museum in memory of the 1905 uprising against the Germans, as a result of which over 250,000 people died of starvation and disease (see the Introduction for the full story). The memorial, sadly, is rarely visited but after a while we managed to find the caretaker to show us round. Athamani was only too pleased to show us everything. Here you can see him holding a shield and club used during the Maji Maji Rebellion.

The cathedral at Peramiho was built about 100 years ago for the Benedictine monks. They still reside here at Peramiho as well as all over Tanzania, but this is their HQ, as it were. The Benedictines are very community-concious and, wherever you go, you will find them working with the people, building, helping with business or revitalising agriculture and more. Peramiho itself is no exception. Here there is a hospital, a secondary school and a trade school.

241

Mbinga, about 100 kms west of Songea, is another centre for coffee in the south. It also now features an enormous Catholic cathedral, almost. By the time you read this it will be finished and quite magnificent. As well as the cathedral, there are many different facilities in the precinct such as accommodation, meeting rooms and a trade school.

The *MV Songea*, a fine example of one of the bigger boats which ply Lake Nyasa. This one has come from Itungi on the northern point of the lake, a short distance west from Matema. It will carry passengers and a wide variety of cargo up and down the lake on the Tanzanian side.

242

When you leave Mbinga and head south-west towards Lake Nyasa, you drive down an escarpment with the most amazing views of the lake. This is Mbamba Bay on Lake Nyasa. A small community that fishes and looks after the few travellers coming in from Malawi.

These fish are *utaka* and are being dried before going up to Songea to sell.

Mbamba Bay is a particular haven of peace: the pace of life is attractive in its gentleness.
This is the pier on the beach made for berthing larger boats from Malawi.

The wide sandy beach at Mbamba Bay is used for drying fishing nets and playing football, as well as being a fine place to relax and enjoy the view.

At the end of the day, as the sun sets over Malawi, life continues its stressful course.

MTWARA

Mtwara region has the Ruvuma river running along its southern border with Mozambique and the region's main towns, Mtwara, Masasi and Newala. Masasi lies at the end of an inexorably long road from Tunduru and is a welcome respite amidst its rocky kopjes. From Masasi you can drive straight to the coast or you can rise up to the Makonde Plateau, through the endless old cashew trees and on to the small town of Newala. From Newala you descend to the coast and to Mtwara, the region's main town.

The region is predominantly peopled by the Makonde. They have strong connections with Mozambique and are well-known for their exquisite carvings, their sizzling *sindimba* drumming and their fine dancing. The Makonde are closely related to the Makua who also live in both Mtwara and Lindi regions. Both groups are matrilineal, tracing their ancestry through the mother. Makonde carvings are virtually as old as the people themselves. In fact, legend has it that the very first Makonde was a carving which came to life. Originally the carvings were used for religious ceremonies, but as the opportunity arose over the years to sell the carvings they started making them with buyers in mind. The Makondes' love of art is deeply felt and one will often see the older Makonde with intricate facial tattoos. Makonde women used to have their upper lip pierced and a wooden plug inserted but the practice of both the tattooing and the lip plug are dying out.

Mtwara, the southernmost region in the country, on the coast, is accessible from Dar es Salaam by boat, or by road across the Rufiji river, although in the rains this road is virtually impassable. There are now plans to rebuild the road and build a bridge over the Rufiji river.

The region is the greatest producer of cashew nuts in the country. They are grown in small plots and the nut grows down the cashew pear and drops off when it matures. The cashew pear is used to make a powerful spirit called 'nippa'. It is illegal to brew or drink it, but still the tradition remains and it is likely that the law was introduced for the benefit of the consumers.

Mtwara town was planned over a huge area and is said to have included a plot for an opera house. This was part of a huge dream for establishing a mechanised groundnut scheme in Nachingwena in the post World War Two years. The planning was inadequate in every way, rainfall was inadequate and the machinery inappropriate for the soil. The scheme collapsed within ten years and at a cost of 35 million pounds. All that was left of the project were three vast tracts of land and a plot to build an opera house.

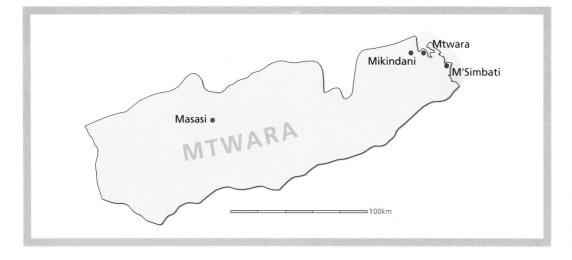

Overleaf: South of Mtwara is a small place called M'Simbati, a small village on a peninsular surrounded by beautiful beaches. M'Simbati is close to the mouth of the Ruvuma river and the Mozambique border.

Masasi town is on the edge of the Makonde Plateau. If you have come from Songea in the west, the most perfect tarmac road is probably the greatest feature of this small oasis. After two solid days of driving on roads that defy the imagination, it is a welcome break and naturally leads you into thinking very kindly about the place. Masasi has a mysterious air about it. The road, the palm trees, the kopje in the background all make for an unusual place.

The Makonde carvings (made from African Blackwood) are famous throughout the world and one of the most popular carvers is Mzee Hendrik Thobias. Seen here carving at his home in Ziwani, south of Mtwara. Mzee Hendrik has taught his son to carve and he himself was taught by his father. The Makonde carvings exhibit one of the most intricate of African carving styles; they often depict family life and the extent of the family and the effect of 'Ujamaa' on the people. The carvings often have a meaning or a story.

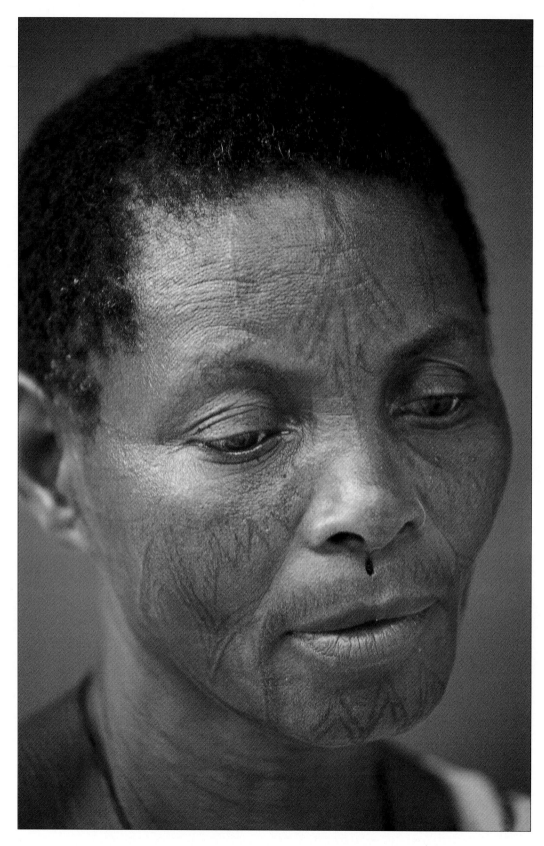

Josephine Emmanuel is a woman of the Makonde tribe and she explained about the traditional scarring: "I lay down on the floor and they cut my face with a sharp knife and rubbed ash into the wounds...." (from the Swahili). You can also see where she used to wear a lip plug on her upper lip. One of the major reasons for the scarring and lip plugs was a preventative measure to stop themselves from being taken as slaves. The slavers would regard them as 'damaged' and would avoid them.

The peace, solitude and tranquility of M'Simbati reigns supreme. Shattered only by the occasional call of the tern, the thud as a coconut hits the sand, the scuttle of a crab across the beach and the blasting of dynamite fishing. Not that it is a problem of course. What is a bit of amazingly beautiful and unique living coral, really! Blast it away. People have to earn a living – but there are better ways of fishing than with dynamite.

254

There are beaches all along the coast of Tanzania and on the islands off the coast, but if it is peace and solitude you want, south of Mtwara is the place.

Mtwara town is a fairly quiet place. It is remote but there is a perceptible coastal bustle. The carvings of the Makonde, the market, the shops, the roads, the buildings and the port all come together to make an interesting provincial capital.

When you drive north from Mtwara along the coast road, about 10 kms outside Mtwara you arrive at Mikindani. This small fishing village has immense character and history. In the town you will find Arab and German buidings, mostly fairly dilapadated, but interesting.

LINDI

Lindi region, considerably bigger than its two coastal region neighbours, stretches a long way inland encompassing a portion of the Selous Game Reserve. The coast of the region is dominated by Lindi and the Kilwas. Lindi town is a peaceful and regularly laid out town with the atmosphere of most coastal towns in Tanzania. The Kilwas, north of Lindi, are made up of three separate places: Kilwa Kivinje, Kilwa Masoko and Kilwa Kisiwani. Kilwa Kivinje is an extraordinarily beautiful small town, to the north of the other two, littered with old buildings and whose people are fishermen and boat builders, using techniques that have been used for centuries. Kilwa Masoko is a modern town which has risen up next to the harbour, from which a small amount of freight is transported along the coast. From the harbour you can get a dhow to take you over the short stretch of water that separates the mainland from Kilwa Kisiwani – in Swahili *kisiwani* means 'the place of the island'. Kilwa Kisiwani is an island of ruins, steeped in history and incredibly interesting to visit.

Kilwa Kisiwani, known in days gone by as only Kilwa, has a great past and was known as "the jewel in the crown of the Zanj coast". As early as AD 1300, Kilwa was the centre of the gold trade. Gold was mined in the kingdom of the Maharanga, in present day Zimbabwe, and either transported overland past Lake Nyasa to Kilwa or taken to the Sofala, in what is now Mozambique, and by dhow to Kilwa. At Kilwa gold was sold to traders and taken to Egypt, Arabia, Persia, India, Thailand, China and the Spice Islands. Archaeological evidence shows that Kilwa managed to mint its own coins and imported expensive porcelain from China and glass from India. In the 14th century, Kilwa became the most prosperous town on the whole East African coast. Its buildings were made of stone and coral and the finest example of this architecture was the Great Mosque and the Great Palace of Kilwa, both on today's Kilwa Kisiwani.

Ibn Batuta visited Kilwa in 1331 and acknowledged the town to be "among the finest and most substantially built in the world".

When Vasco da Gama came to Kilwa in 1498, the people of Kilwa made it abundantly clear that he was not welcome. The Portuguese came again in 1505 demanding tribute from Kilwa. They refused and the island was ransacked and more than three-quarters of its people killed or forced to flee. Kilwa's glory had already started to wane when, in 1587, a horde of cannibals called the Zimba from the Zambezi region crossed over from the mainland in the middle of the night, with the help of a traitor, and slayed and ate the town's entire population, estimated to have been about 3,000. That was the end of Kilwa's days of glory.

Today the Makonde, Makua and Mwera are the dominant people in the region. Cashew nuts are one of the cash crops and cassava, rice, maize and beans are also grown. Coconuts also thrive well along the coast and around Lindi town there is salt still in production.

Not far south of Lindi there are a few salt works such as this. The shallow square pans are dug, filled with sea water and then, about a month later, the water has evaporated and the salt is collected, bagged and sold.

Lindi town is beautifully situated on the shores of the Indian Ocean and on a natural harbour, which makes life easier for the many fishermen in the town.

Two fishermen, Mussa Muhamed and Ahmed
Omari, spend the afternoon fixing a few small leaks
in the cracks of their wooden canoe.

Selimani Mfaome sells Kolekole in the fish
market in Lindi. The stiff green bristled brush
is for the de-scaling of the fish.

Kilwa Kivinje is one of the most extraordinary places I visited in the entire country. It remains as it has been for decades undisturbed by the devastating progress of man.

In Kilwa Kivinje I was clearly a visitor yet while I wandered the alleys, waterfront and streets people would be delighted to greet and chat for a while, pass the time of day, talk about the state of the fishing, remembering the past which all the Kilwas are steeped in and make a visitor feel genuinely welcome.

Occasionally, one realises that developments and the rapid availability of everything in life can make us miss the point entirely. Life ought to be more about relationships and feelings than about economics or politics

To be more like the people of Kilwa Kivinje with their human values, reminding ourselves what and who is really important, we might have a chance of waking up in the morning and being happy with who we are.

Opposite: Ndoka Husseini Ndoka shows one of the more peculiar catches of the day, a sea slug. He also greatly enjoyed showing me that when you squeeze them, out springs a jet of water.

The small streets of Kilwa Kivinje are lined with amazing old buildings dating back to Omani times, when Kilwa Kivinje was a centre for the slave trade.

The boat builder in the blue boiler suit is Muhammed Shea who has been making
dhows since 1972. He, like many of the craftsmen in Tanzania, was taught the trade by
his father. He said it usually takes him about 18 days to build a dhow of this size. He
has about 10 days to go on this one.

Kilwa Masoko, a few kilometres past Kilwa Kivinje on the tarmac road, is a small village fairly typical of anywhere in Tanzania. Still very warm and welcoming with a beach just outside and a smattering of Baobab trees on it. Kilwa Masoko is also the departure point for trips to Kilwa Kisiwani.

The market in Kilwa Masoko sells clothes as well as fish and other foods and all the bits and pieces that life requires. I was particulaly drawn to the philosophy of the purple T-shirt at the end on the right-hand side, so I bought it.

To reach the historic island of Kilwa Kisiwani, which actually means 'Kilwa On The Island', we took a dhow across the short stretch of sea and mangroves between the island and the mainland. On the outward leg we went alongside some mangroves in order to get into a position to tack – or something like that – and so our main form of forward propulsion was Mpunga and his crew. I think the motor was being serviced.

265

The first building you see when you reach Kilwa Kisiwani is the Portugese *gereza* or prison. It wasn't actually used as a prison; it was used as a fort. Built by the Omani Arabs around 1800, it also incorporates the walls of a smaller Portugese fort built in 1505. The thick walls are made of coral.

Opposite: Kilwa Kisiwani is a treasure island of ancient ruins and sadly, as always, there is never enough space to show a fraction of it. You'll have to go there yourself and see it. Ask for Mpunga; he'll take you across the channel from Kilwa Masoko for a very reasonable rate! On the island you will find ruins dating back to the 14th and 15th centuries. These arches are in the Great Mosque or Friday Mosque, as prayers were held on Fridays. The mosque was built in the 14th century and would have played a vital role in the community. It would have held up to 600 worshippers at one time.

Pwani

Pwani, meaning 'coast' in Swahili, is a region that covers the middle part of the Tanzanian coast, with the exception of the small Dar es Salaam region in the centre. This area has been frequently mentioned in ancient travel books and stretches along the Indian Ocean coast of Tanzania from a little north of the town of Sadani to just south of the delta of River Rufiji.

Rufiji river together with its tributaries – the main ones being the Great Ruaha, the Luwengu and Kilombero rivers – form the largest catchment in the whole of East Africa. The mouth of the Rufiji has the biggest mangrove forest in the world.

The Rufiji river practically divides the south from the north coast of Tanzania and anyone travelling to the southern regions of Lindi and Mtwara or going to Dar es Salaam from the south must cross it by ferry. Presently, the Government has announced plans to build a tarmac road from Kibiti in Pwani region across a bridge over the Rufiji to Lindi and Mtwara.

Directly opposite the mouth of the Rufiji river is mainland Tanzania's biggest Indian Ocean island archipelago, Mafia. The archipelago includes: Mafia, the biggest, Jibondo, Chole, Juani and Koma. Around the islands is some of Tanzania's best diving and fishing. They also have their own history as evident from the various ruins scattered around them.

North of Dar region is Bagamoyo, the coastal town that featured so prominently in the slave trade and was called Bagamoyo or *Bwaga-moyo* which is the Swahili equivalent of 'dash-down-and-shatter-your-heart' when

you reach Bagamoyo because shortly you will be auctioned and sold and taken away in dhows and ships across the sea, never to see your native land again. Bagamoyo, smash down your heart.

The regional headquarters of Pwani region are in Kibaha, a new town that has been established along the Dar es Salaams Morogoro road. Kibaha is one of the towns shaded by the largest number of trees in Tanzania.

Pwani region is mainly the land of small-scale farmers. Cashew nuts are grown as the major cash crop, but rice, maize, beans and vegetables are grown for a ready market in Dar es Salaam.

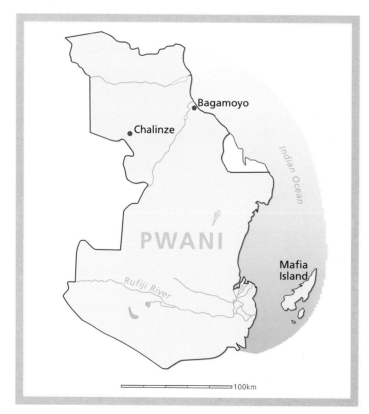

Pwani is reputedly the land of the Swahili people. Heated debate has been going on as to whether the Swahili are a distinct ethnic group. Those who argue for their existence say that the people with no language or vernacular other than the Swahili language and without any culture other than the Swahili culture must *be* the Swahili, the 'owners' of the language. Others, arguing against this reasoning, say that present-day Swahili is the mother tongue of most children born of Tanzanian parents from different ethnic groups. They point out that Swahili language and culture has spread beyond the narrow coastal borders and is now used by most Tanzanians as their first language, and their numbers grow with the dying of ethnic culture and loyalties.

The Rufuji River, which flows through the Selous Game Reserve, must be crossed to reach Dar from the south. It is hit or miss whether or not the ferry is working. Fortunately is was working when we were there. The Rufiji Delta is reputedly the largest mangrove forest in the world.

Flying off the coast south of Dar, you realise how many islands there must be. This is Koma Island not far north of Mafia Island.

Most of the islands in the Mafia archipelago are surrounded by mangrove trees as opposed to sand beaches. This mangrove crab is one of the residents.

On Chole Island, the third largest island in the Mafia archipelago, as on Jibondo Island the second largest island, there are many ruins. These date back to the Shirazi era in the 12th century.

Fishing is the main occupation of the people of the Mafia archipelago. These fish and fish strips are drying so they can be stored or sold.

The shore of Chole Island, which is Mafia Island's close neighbour, reveals the history of the area in the form of the ruins of a church several hundred years old, dating from the Omani era.

Overleaf: With Mafia Island at the back and a couple of small satellite islands, the dhow makes the picture complete when viewed from 2000 feet.

On Chole Island you can find a variety of peculiar wildlife. This is the epauletted fruit bat.

North of Dar is the old port of Bagamoyo. It gained infamy in the 19th century for being the centre of the slave trade. Subsequently, it was an important base for the Germans. However since the Germans left it has not had the opportunity to develop much. The history of Bagamoyo is evident throughout the town. This monument and buildings are part of the Catholic Mission. The Mission was opened in 1868 by the Holy Ghost Fathers. Their mission in life was fighting slavery and the Mission acted as a home for ransomed slaves. The Fathers would buy slaves, mainly children, following the constitution of their missionary congregation: "To fight slavery by ransoming as many slaves as possible."

The beach at Bagamoyo.

In 1981 the Government of Tanzania established the Bagamoyo College of Art. The college teaches traditional dance and music, modern dance and music, drama, fine art, acrobatics, stage technology, art and society and art and management. It is the only college of its type anywhere in East and Central Africa. If this photograph is anything to go by, they also study philosophy.

Boats are not always moored on the beach; occasionally they are anchored off-shore depending on the tides.

ZANZIBAR
UNGUJA & PEMBA ISLANDS

Zanzibar is an archipelago that is made up of two major islands: Unguja – which has also been called Zanzibar – and Pemba. Pemba was part of the mainland in Pliocene times about 15 million years ago, but Unguja was separated from the mainland during the Quaternary geological upheavals, a mere one million years ago. The sea that separates the islands from the mainland – about 50km wide for Pemba and 30km for Unguja – was more responsible for bringing Zanzibar closer to the mainland coast than for keeping the islands apart. For thousands of years, Zanzibar was the gateway to the mainland coasts and its hinterland, and an active partner to a rich and complex international trade that included China and Japan, Thailand, Burma, the spice islands of Malaysia and Indonesia, India, Sri Lanka, the Maldives Islands, Persia, Arabia, Egypt and the Middle East, as well as the Mediterranean world. As part of the East African coast, Zanzibar was known to traders and seafarers and the Unguja Island is thought to be the island of Menouthias mentioned in the *Periplous of the Erythræn Sea* a book written around AD 110 by a Greek traveller describing trade in the Indian Ocean. A trading settlement called Qanbalu, reputedly the earliest recorded trading post on the East African coast, was on Pemba Island in the year 1000.

From the earliest historical times, Zanzibar was a confluence of two cultural influences: that of the indigenous people, mainly Bantu, whom the Arab and Persian visitors called the 'Zanj'; and that of outsiders, mainly from the Persian Gulf. Islam was brought to Zanzibar around 630 AD mainly by people who originated from Shiraz on the Persian Gulf. These people, known as the Shirazi, initially settled as traders around Mogadishu on the Banadir coast, but later moved south to Zanzibar and to other places on the East African coast. The Bantu hosts emulated their visitors' way of life and religion. As trade grew, the language of the hosts had to accommodate trading concepts and the new values that were more cosmopolitan than the Bantu culture. That language had also to accommodate the diversity in the cultural melting pot of the East African coast. That language was Swahili.

Today, Zanzibar is a separate state within Tanzania and is dependant on the export of herbs and spices, in particular cloves – 90% of which are grown on Pemba Island – and tourism. The main food crops of Zanzibar are rice, maize, millet, cassava, bananas and coconuts. Zanzibar has a great number of coconut trees and the coconuts are exported as copra or coconut oil and the fibres that cover the coconut shells are used locally for making ropes, mats and bags. Other exports include cocoa and chilli peppers.

One of the aspects of Zanzibar which make it so exotic are the incredible diversity of people inhabiting the islands, such as the Pembans of Pemba Island, the Tumbatu of Tumbatu Island and northern Unguja Island, the Hadimu of central and southern Unguja and in general the Bantu, Arab, Indian, Mauritanian, Seychellois and Madagascan people.

Today Zanzibar offers the visitor an opportunity to explore a remarkable history or to walk along its sandy beaches, drinking coconut milk and relaxing. However you want to spend your time on the islands they will reward you with a very special experience.

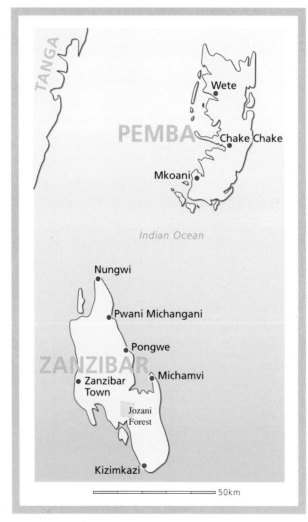

As you approach Zanzibar Town on Unguja Island, you try to empty your mind of everything you have heard about it. Better to enter this museum town and land on the island with a clear mind, unbiased by an unhappy traveller or an over-enthusiastic resident. So much is heard about this place it is virtually impossible to give it a chance to show you itself. I wanted to give it a chance.

Christ Church Cathedral in Zanzibar Town. It was built between 1873 and 1880 on the site of the slave market. There is a wooden crucifix next to the pulpit which was made from the tree next to which Dr. Livingstone's heart was buried. The altar in the Cathedral is actually on the site of the old slave whipping post.

Zanzibar produces a lot of herbs and spices and there is one particulaly enterprising gentleman who has established a company which sells herbs, spices, oils and other similar products. He is called 'Madawa', which means Medicines, because he uses his great knowledge of herbs and spices to make remedies and cures for various ailments. This is his workshop, where they are bottling a herbal massage oil.

Stone Town is well known for its narrow streets.

The intricately carved doors in Zanzibar used to be a sign of the owners wealth or status. The more intricate the door, the wealthier the owner of the house. The studs on the doors probably originate from Persia or India where they discouraged elephants from knocking them down. This is not a common threat in Stone Town at the moment; the studs are decorative.

In Pongwe, on the beach, out of the sun, Ibrahim is making a fish trap. The trap takes him about a week to build completely. It has a funnel entrance with loose pieces at the end which means the fish can get in but not out. The trap is loaded with a few rocks to weigh it down, bait is put in and then it is lowered into the sea and left overnight. Ibrahim reckoned it was a handy way of fishing.

Public transport on the island is mostly this type of bus or *dala-dala*. It is remarkable how laid-back they are here. It is usually chaos catching a bus anywhere, but things were much calmer here.

On the beach at Pwani Mchangani we noticed a few bovine visitors. There was something unusual about seeing a group of cows plodding along a beautiful sandy beach, not eating or drinking, just taking a stroll.

Seaweed farming was introduced to Zanzibar around 1989 as another source of income for the local people. Seaweed cuttings are tied to strings underwater, which are attatched to the sticks. They are left for about a week and then collected from the sea and dried in the sun. Seaweed is sold to exporters who send it abroad to be used in toothpaste, cosmetics and other products. On the east coast there has been some quarrelling between local people and hotels because the hotels claim that the seaweed farms are unsightly and it discourages the tourists to swim. The people claim that they need the extra money from the seaweed to improve their standard of living. Fair one.

The welcoming face of Zanzibar.

This road leads down into Pwani Mchangani.

Up in the northern part of Unguja Island is a small village called Nungwi. It is the centre for dhow building on the island. Haji Mussa Ali, seen here using a tradtional drill, is in charge of making this dhow. It will take about one month to finish with three people working on it.

In Nungwi a few fishermen sort out the net in preparation for a fishing trip.

Unguja Island

As Nungwi is the northernmost point on Unguja Island there are both east and west coasts.
This out-rigger canoe basks in the last rays of the sun on the west coast.

When you head back south, somewhere in the middle you will come across this extraordinary palm tree. Surprisingly it is called Twisted Palm.

Jozani Forest is the last remnant of indigenous forest which used to cover much of the central part of the island. It has been protected since 1952 and gazetted as a nature reserve since 1960. It contains a diverse selection of wildlife, including the Blue monkey, Ader's duiker, the suni, leopard and Kirk's red colobus. Most of these animals – apart from the monkeys – are very shy, so unless you have a lot of time and patience you are unlikely to meet them. What you are likely to see, though, is Kirk's red colobus, *Colobus badius kirkii*, pictured here.

Head to the southern part of the island to Kizimkazi. There are two Kizimkazis; Kizimkazi
Dimbani and Kizimkazi Mkunguni, about 2 kilometres apart. The old mosque in Kizimkazi
Dimbani dates back to 12th century Shirazi times. Kizimkazi Mkunguni (shown here) boasts a
marvellous beach.

Taking a boat from Kizimkazi Mkunguni was a great experience. The colour of the sea completely inimitable – as was our guide, Ahmed or Rastaman (he had lots of hair under his woolly hat). Ahmed takes a break from the stresses and toils of life.

Dhow and Stone Town.

Unguja Island

Left: Michamvi is on the west coast of the head-land which sticks out opposite Chwaka, about halfway up the Island on the east coast. Here a young lad approaches us with a business proposition. After a little bit of negotiating we agreed on a price for a couple of coconuts and so up went our new pal, Muhammed. He climbed up the immensely tall tree apparently effortlessly, except when he got halfway up and the T-shirt he had tied around his feet for extra grip fell off! However, business is business and he wasn't in the least bit put out.

Right: Muhammed is somewhere in the top of the middle palm tree. You can see the coconuts on their way earthwards.

Safely back to earth Muhammed orders me to take a picture of him like so; being of such a nervous disposition I couldn't possibly refuse.

295

Pemba Island is about 3 hours by quick boat from Unguja Island. The island is very different from Unguja Island in many ways, the most obvious of which is the far smaller number of visitors. This, however, offers the traveller the opportunity to experience the island all by yourself. Chake Chake is the main town on the island. It is a great place, small in comparison to Zanzibar Town, but very peaceful with an interesting diversity of architecture. This is one of the old German buidings in Chake Chake.

Abra and Juma were very happy to introduce me to their shop in Chake Chake. Juma, on the right, told me that it was interesting meeting visitors because they don't get many here.

Off the west coast of Pemba is Misali Island. This is a small but exceptional island surrounded by amazing coral formations, pictured here out of the water. Apparently the reef around Misali offers some of the best diving in the region.

Misali Island is also the home for a small community of fishermen. Some of today's catch, squid, being hung out to dry.

Pemba Island

Pemba has an infrastructure which comes as a bit of a surprise as it is considered a backwater by those who don't know it. This signpost is in the north of Pemba.

In the north of Pemba is a long beach called Vumawimbe (Loud Waves). Here we found a few fishermen pulling in a net from what seemed like miles out at sea. It took ages to get the net in and they were rewarded with only a few small fish. After I had been chatting to them and taking pictures while they were slaving away, they were highly entertained when my conscience got the better of me and I wrapped my Nikons around my neck and started pulling. Just a little contribution, that's all. They all found it very funny and were laughing so much that they were scarcely able to do anything! I was only trying to help.

This beach is called Malindi and it is next to the village of Maziwa Ngombe (Cow's Milk) on the east coast. Here the nets are laid out ready for the next fishing trip.

Pemba Island

These islands in the Indian Ocean are not just
tropical paradises. This is a housing estate in
Mkoani on the southern tip of Pemba Island.

Both of the major islands in Zanzibar have a
sizeable herb and spice industry. It is Pemba
Island, though, which exports the vast majority
of cloves from Zanzibar. These are recently harvested cloves which will be dried for a few days,
depending on the weather, and then sold to the
central purchasing office in Chake Chake.

Haraka haraka haina baraka
Great haste has no blessing

Bibliography

Africa Encyclopedia, *Oxford University Press* 1974

A history of East Africa, *Atiero Odhiambo E.S.; Ouso T.I.; Williams J.F.M.* Longman Group Ltd. 1988

Tanzania: a Political Economy, *Coulson A.* Clarendon Press 1985

A Guide to Kenya and Northern Tanzania, *Horrobin D.F.* East African Publishing House 1971

Modern Tanzanians: a volume of biographies. *Liffe J.* East African Publishing House 1973

Footprints in the Ashes of Time, *Leakey M.D.* National Geographic Vol 155, No.4 April 1979

Mwalimu: the influence of Nyerere on Britain, *Legurn C. and Mman G,* Tanzania Society 1995

Custodians of the Land - Ecology and culture in the history of Tanzania, *Maddox G. Giblin, J and Kimambo I.N.,* East African Studies 1996

East Africa - An introductory history, *Maxon R.M.* East African Educational Publishers 1994

East Africa: its peoples and resources, *Morgan W.T.W.* Oxford University Press 1975

History of East Africa, *Reusch R.* Evong. Missionsverlag G.M.B.H. Stuttgart 1954

East Africa through a thousand years, *Were G.S. and Wilson D.A.* Evans Brothers Limited 1975

The Bradt Guide to Tanzania, *Philip Briggs* 1997

The Behaviour Guide to African Mammals, *Richard Despard Estes.* Russel Friedman Books 1995